CW00507267

CONTENTS

Travesty	3
Chapter Two	18
Chapter Three	24
Chapter Four	40
Chapter Five	54
Chapter Six	89
Chapter Seven	96
The End	107

TRAVESTY

Starting a new book is easier than it seems as far as ideas go and rarely, very rarely ends up being a boring or arduous task at times. Regarding self worth and the worth of your Muse i.e. the person or soul closest to you whilst writing. To write as I am here, in a descriptive way, Its more personal and enjoyable for the reader, less self-conscious for me, which makes dreaming the future easier, that's what I think. I'm definitely a dreamer yknow? I kinda live to dream, but dreaming needs dreamers, that's you and your dreams your ideas and your open honest beliefs whomever you are and what's going on in your life right now. Are you always chasing friends and love, always sensitive to the energy of others, always wanting to be in the moment and enjoy the heart of the moment?

Up and over, what's next and why? Who's coming into your life now and why? Where's the good? The good people? Do they think being distant keeps them safe, do they feel like I'm some kind of conquistador and I'm doing it all for them? Of course they do. Don't you remember those silent promises made in school, in the back of your mind over the formative years of your life of honor and loyalty and truth? I do. That's your human Heart at its best, making plans for us all when were together, growing up as one well intuitive unified collective conscious gang of knights and angels promising the world and all it has in it. Were brave and we know what time it is, where were at and how good it feels to be young, free and ready for anything. Whamo! Anything does come slamming in our front doors at a fierce pace indeed, first cigarette, first kiss, first hangover, first joint, first love, that's a biggie, if you're like me, lucky (touch wood!)My first love lasts forever and I always think of her as one eternal friend that is always there for me and always will be. Her smiling face, her joy, her fun, her mature attitude as a soul-mate. Last Kiss.

Resilience is one of the many meanings of life. As a resilient person I find my place in the world is very different than other non-helpful resilient Bastardos as I like to call them. Resilient bastardos heard our silent promises, eaves-dropped so to say on our Cosmic serenade with destiny, when we made our pacts with our friend's subconscious collective private minds. Our life's destiny mapped out clearly after years of character development and life experiences that slowly began to take shape and develop into some kind of enigmatic plan. Why one person always lucked out when it came to trouble. Trouble and connection, connections and coincidences that became a habit, or was it fate? Destined to be a criminal regarding the interchanging coincidence of life-changing energies. Boom! One minute you're cool and the gang, the next you're nicked for cheating on an exam or worse, you're put up a level and are seen as a genius because of cheating and are now in the swats class, Hell! It happens, it happened to me. Don't worry I flunked honors math's rapidly and was sent back to the rebellious chaps soon enough but not before I realized that the swats where ok. Not too dumb after all, just nerds, realizing that we (the rebels) were destined for karma big-time! I knew it then that after being stuck with the same bunch of freaks since baby infants that we never had the chance of sanity. Together from five years old till seventeen, a close bunch of loopers only knowing fun and frolics, never seeing the light of learning, never knowing calm or study. It was always about the jokes and the camaraderie, plus we knew that Bohemia was ours for the taking, by the age of thirteen we were already to become the next Gods of rock, or of the art world or literature or any kind of rebel you can name. Although nearing important exams we crammed like elephants to get reasonable grades, its only math's that was the painful subject. Not that any one of us ever needed algebra, like ever! We realized the crock this world is made of and wanted to rule and reign like kings above it all. The positive energy of youth, never-ending, never tiring, always moving forewords. That's passion, that's energy and no life-lessons stand in the way. They can't, you can't get in the way of progress, we are the generation of ground-breakers and we know it. Self-realization, it's what it's all about, its inevitably Universal, not personal, that's why there are so many casualties, we think we are destined for something, we are, our fate. Our fate can be our destiny, even if we end up becoming the anti-hero, challenging accepted norms, like struggling artist verses doctor (they even get a capital letter) but that doesn't make them intelligent emotionally or spiritually! Struggling artist verses squares; art begins to rebel against squareness and the futility of urban existence. Art begins to exist in relation to ignorance instead of celebrating life it begins to celebrate death, an equal and opposite reaction to societies norms. Where's the self-realization gone? Down the swanny, people start to think that life is about rebelling against being controlled instead of taking control. Who takes control instead? Corporate bodies, governments, banks, the rich boring old anachronisms of past ideals going nowhere but to wage war on recovering third-world countries that control the gold or the political situations. Where are the youth? Doing what they always do, falling into the same ideals they always do, reaction. React to the world at large, to the emotional stunting of our communities, react, react, and react. That's the way it's supposed to be when humanity is still developing from the cave to the Space-Race. But we are the Space-Race, at least as good as it's going to get for now and maybe forever the way things are going, so what's up? What's up is way too big a picture for most people to fathom. That this could be as far as we can go, for now, that's why we appear to be going backwards in many ways. No Nukes? Ok, let's try anarchy, chaos; take a look at the Middle East, anarchy enough for you, chaotic energies enough? Yes, that's enough for me thanks what else is on. Well we have chilled-out Buddhism on channel four with a low-fat mocha with whipped-cream and some greatly talented artistic melancholy followed by some Hollywood blockbusters with cherry-soda on the side.

What a world! Indeed, here one minute gone the next, to where? Who knows, but still a plan is a plan for some of us and plans sometimes need planning rather than relying on luck. Luck can turn sour, believe me, so where to now? Chase the moola, the game is on and always about the money honey. Love is enough when you have a life, a love, a lover or just friends. To get by and keep going down that road, unless, unless for some extra-terrestrial reason your life begins to appear more like a labyrinth, or a maze. Labyrinths serve a purpose when we're up against the unshurity of other peoples beliefs in relation to us. Where the pieces fit in regarding fate and the hand it deals both you and other people. For me being privileged from birth helped a lot, although I have always thought that God had led my parents and theirs to higher ground for being good and not getting caught by mistakes. Mistakes perhaps that our adversaries families have not avoided, the blame game. That's a mistake that makes a game of blame, for them, the people we call our enemies or bullies or complainants want our place in the world. "They" think we don't fit into their delusional reality, a reality built on blame. If they think we are to blame for their family's failure in life or because they receive the thought that we can be blamed for their underprivileged status then they can move on this and use blame like a weapon to be dealt to privileged victims like us. They have a status complex. It's all relative and fits the usual delinquent mind to listen to the un- reasonable voice in their heads that rich or well off people haven't earned their place in the World. Of course we have, that's destiny, and it's our destiny not to have a complex but to realize our situation and fight back. Beat the bullies by being brave, use reason with unreasonable thugs or fight back with might. Might is right when righteousness is on your side and Bullies serve a purpose, they teach us about etiquette, what's right or wrong, what's purposefully built into the needy person, the person that needs, respect, that doesn't get any at home, so bullies at school, or in life to feel that that's the reason they are ignored at home or wherever- to be trained to pull down the more privileged people and get revenge on them. Revenge is just jealousy hiding behind a mask. Bullies are naturally bred to be jealous or embarrassed at their lot in life, they begin to see a reason behind everything, that they are being tested by us to defend us from being abused by a system that fails. The system of life doesn't fail, but for them it has, apparently, so we become their teachers in regards as we are the victims of greed and ignorance, especially if we believe in God. We need to be educated as to the law of the jungle where only the fittest survive, get it? If we are privileged then we are greedy and must succumb to their twisted philosophy that they are the strongest and we are weak, weakened by being soft and easily manipulated. So we need to be helped by them, at first it's just an idea, they think of it, and decide to employ this idea and after the first try, it begins, the action that becomes a reaction. Reactions to us, we are ill-prepared for in youth that can follow us all our lives until we see what's behind the people who drag us down or who blame us for everything and get their day or have their way. Who are they? They are our sharpening stones, our teachers, our enemies that become our allies because by the time we become adults, we will be experienced enough to know how to deal with the bigger fish. The people who have become our nemesi, or as an individual, our nemesis. "Ah come on" they will say, but as they say so are positioning themselves for the big kill. The name calling at school that going unpunished will manifest in adult years and destroy character and reputation. If it's a class system at work then it becomes a national issue. Very touchy subject and hard not to offend the wrong people i.e. the people doing the offending. For example a fascist believes their intended victim deserves no less than death or worse. What's behind that fascist? What life-force drives them and collectively what does it represent? It represents politics, the personal politics of the individual, their beliefs and more importantly their needs. They need to take, because it's being offered by those that represent fascist beliefs. Privileged people are usually good because they don't need to take, by force or by swindle, for any reason, their privileged and probably deserve to be so. Not rich or spoiled just regular middleclass people. Not to generalize, working class people can be just as good but they understand my plight because they live in the thick of it, where the fittest do survive and they know it. There's a ladder on one side and snakes on the other, I didn't write the rules, it's just the way it is. The way it is for some, for others its worse because their situation is worse, with little or no hope of goodness or equality, possibly living in deprived areas far away from the cities or towns. Good people in many ways but where do privileged people fit in? They don't and that's my point. It's all in; as far as delusions of grandeur are concerned and we become victims by proxy.

Class systems are in place and have been since the dawn of time. Where one creature has and one has not, or territory makes animals of us all. The meaning of life is to be human and humane. Not so easy if cause and effect deal you a heavy blow and only family can be blamed. Seek and yea shall find, or search and destroy, there's the two sides of the coin and sometimes the two merge into one. Our brains are even made of the stuff, grey matter. Where good and evil meet, where we decipher what's good for us or what's sometimes necessary for survival i.e. drugs, booze, nicotine, physical needs or desires, it's a long list but it originates from need. The need for energy or the need to dull the pain of adolescence that becomes a habit like smoking, or an addiction like smoking. You can get used to addictions and as they become necessary stables of our lives we begin to compromise. For our needs, but what of the need to see, the reasons for our needs, the emotions that cause our systems to need crutches. Oh we remember the thoughts surrounding us before that first cigarette, but in the moment it was just for the buzz and it was character building. It did define us as individuals because it was something we could control. Nobody could stop us at the time and we knew we could hide from prying eyes to do it. Freedom! Now when it comes to blame, I attract it because I'm to blame, if I can be singled out and caught out by appearing prejudiced, except I already appear prejudiced. I'm aware of the fact and only because I can sympathize with them that truly are, prejudiced that is. I sympathize with them to know them, to feel their pain, to approach their sensitivities with an understanding of that technique I described earlier, the cause that dealt them their affliction, to become a victim, to identify with being a victim. Victims of fate, of families place in the world, victims of pride and nationalistic beliefs. Troubadours of excuse and unreasonable delusion, fake delusion though fed on foundations of panicked sympathetic intuitive anxiety. Power indeed that starts in childhood and develops into immature-adult action upon the world at large, the jungle.

We are forced to see the world through the eyes of people that live in relation to us. Their opinions are formed by their reactions to our place in the world. By losing their place and finding themselves mixed in with people outside of their neighborhood or world. How did they get here, where are they going, who knows? The people that put them there, our forefathers. Our forefathers, ancestor's e.t.c. who could have dealt with politics better in the past but didn't have the chance or the foresight to learn how to deal with other people. How to communicate with other people without being hooked by their sensitivities, and blamed for the outcome. High-maintenance bodies. The truth is that I could go on and on describing why we are the way we are but at the end of the day destruction usually isn't construction, war doesn't change anything, it gives us faster cars, more industrialization, more boundaries, less moral boundaries and a load of fat-cats telling us that War is good. Within reason and also sacrifice is good, taxes, charges, fines, fees e.t.c. Perhaps collective consciousness is God. Perhaps the reason alternate life-forms exist is to pool representations of Universal laws together. The Universe is energy ultimately so therefore it has to be represented by energy. So, how? Creation of lifeforms that represent difference. Varieties of difference serving a purpose, expansion of life. Otherwise we would all be one with the origin of life as pure white light with a single Soul as its nucleus. Simple singular and safe, maybe with an exact opposite being a Black-Hole, anti-life-force. Each with a single purpose, existence. Coming together after Eons of discovery and chaotic manipulation of energies represented via creation, natural selection and chance or destiny or divine intervention. We cannot see ourselves as anything but white or grey or black from one moment to the next depending on the role we are playing at that moment. No more examples. Eventually Black-Hole meets pure white light and they become nothing. Bending through space-time, never meeting but forming a connection perfectly. Perfections beyond our mortal bodies but not our spirit-soul body. That's where all life exists in the spirit; everything else is categorized by illusive reality i.e. the illusion that were here at all. But were here that's for sure, there's only one reality, everything else is energies experimenting with possibility. One defined reality for all and everything with an extension of more but limited expansion. That's what defines our character and personal choices, limitation and exploration. We all basically need love and attention as beings designed for love and attention. We are privileged to know that human compassion is necessary for responsible beings i.e. you I hope. I want good people to read this and I hope you are good, good natured well-bred youthful exiting powerful creative people. I am. Concentrating on constructive ideas and slowly learning to allow destructive personas to be watched peripherally so we can show them that they are not interested in our Utopian ideals. Whatsoever!

Allow yourself to float into positive thinking; hey it's easier after taking some St John's Wort capsules like I have. No wonder negativity is falling away. I feel better already. Yes it's a copout and I need it. For myself being sensitive to stress and pressure I have to take something to quell the anger I feel and because of the negative energy around us all today. We all need love and attention and where we find it defines not only ourselves but where half the population representing goodness gets it too. I believe that if Yin-yang, black and white, day and night, Good and Evil are equal and opposite then so too do the people of Earth have to be. Each of us good people, in some way, but some more than others. For each of us there is a general consensus in relation to who is bad and who is good and why. It's easier to explain by using toddlers as examples, because we are in many ways just children and are created by spirits in bodies who can pass on their traits to their spawn, as they do. Some New Age philosophies say there are twelve types of people, twelve Star signs; this idea is connected to truth as far as good technique is concerned. They're only trying to utilize this idea because they need something, some tool to do so. We all need tools to utilize our ideals, it helps, yes were aware that it's just a temporary solution but isn't it exiting wondering how close we are to the truth and that there are indeed a limited number of personalities out there. I find now that the clearer my head the clearer I see this simple philosophy is indeed probably the closest to a good workable one. Regarding usage in defining categories and the way people are categorized by the powers that be. Think about it, corporate bodies and rich men are characterized by their personalities and utilized by mostly destructive negative energy (usually, generally) for generally the same reasons. Need for emotional satisfaction in relation to their reactions living in a loveless world i.e. they need to fill the void within with self-satisfying Ego-filling substitutes, cigar-smoking, abuse of power e.t.c. all attention seekers. Who cares? The environment, which we are connected to? We are responsible for the weakest links in our humanity, the rich people the consumers the irresponsible destructive industrialization of Mother-Earth. She's for sale! But whose buying her and who suffers, we all do. Don't worry Aliens believe that all life is relative and we can create new worlds for God and country on other planets, perhaps they're right. Still here we are looking for new planets, good little servants for the new Cosmic race, rich and poor. In the meantime we can't fall out of sync, we have our own lives to think of and how we fit in, in all of this. We do actually or can do make a huge difference by realizing, realizing what's going on, outside of the self-serving immature peer-pressure related society we live in and come from. But once the philosopher twice the hermit, trying to find a higher ground means fighting against the powers that have helped create our society and its dogma. Heavy stuff for your impressionable open-minded grey-matter? Maybe, maybe, plus do you believe in aliens? Even so can you let them exist around you in spirit? Aliens? Why not keep talking about the class system, I was interested, well you see the class system is an integral part of our society and plays a huge part in our lives except its meaningless. Figuring out other people's problems with you, is a waste of time and yet all important as to why they have a problem at all. Our weaknesses offer people what they think is opportunity, human beings have weaknesses and weak people see these as opportunity to exact revenge on us. Status complex is a genetic muscle-memory of sorts, it stifles our superior ability to rise above our petty Ego and self-preservation. Also having enemies helps us to avoid weakness and study ourselves from the perspective of cause and effect. Whatever, life will sort you out eventually you'll start to see the supermen and women in your lives, as sure as the Idiots too.

Standing aside for a minuit and looking at the bigger picture, does their status give them a complex? Ohh yea baby! I'm feelin it now ok. Being born into a life directly created as potentially life-changing people we have the right and the need to overcome obstacles rather than create them. It's a metaphor (If I have to explain it, please stop reading and go back to your impotent lives) pun aside, it's a metaphor. Overcoming the obstacles that attribute themselves to cause and effect for example, "The World is round" We are led to believe that, but is it? If we believe there are other plains on this world then they must be perceived visually. In our heads, clear positive constructive ones for creating a fill in whatever Hole needs filling. Plains of consciousness for the everyman, poor or rich, privileged with normal parents, there has to be an equal balance of good and bad, so the privilege is chance and chance is closest to change. Millennium awakening, ever travelled, in your mind with the purpose involved of seeing your home, in your head from your workplace e.t.c. Seeing your home in your mind's eye and having rapid subconscious thoughts regarding any number of connections or needs, like coming home safe or having your midweek meal of whatever's happening in your head during this supposed daydream which is in fact an astral connection and the beginnings of telekinesis or psychic connection to mother, friends or family. Or being afraid of getting home because of inherent anxieties from childhood of always being in trouble. We all invent other worlds of consciousness in our minds for different reasons. We develop gifts of perception but are they illusion or reality is it all in our heads or can we really leave our bodies and travel the astral plane (rhetorical) Touching other places "In Spirit" Yes we can, or maybe it's an illusion, or a bit of both or neither! Who knows really, after body-life will tell us all we needed to know about being human but couldn't see why or how e.t.c. Getting the picture? We can learn but still were just examples of our own existence as compared to the real thing. The truth is that it doesn't matter that psychic abilities exist; it's the heart of the matter that matters. People get so messed up and confused trying to figure things out mentally that they forget what they already knew. We all have spiritual connections to our families; we see them in our minds eye naturally through natural spiritual gifts. The psychic developments we are used to developing, we mostly all already have, subconsciously and consciously. Learning to be in-tune with our emotional and mental selves reminds us that we are already able to see and hear other peoples distant selves, people far away are close to us and think of us with their whole self. They tune-in to us when they think of us and feel our presence when they do, normal and natural no funny noises or dramatic psychic phenomenon just our human condition when were at one with ourselves and healthy and whole. Higher destinies await us of course but the reason for existence has to be tied in with the reason for having a reason, were here and what's happening is love, life, and living, everything else comes second. Work struggle and healing life's hurts. Healing hurts and aftershock, that means having a purpose regarding responsibility. Healing the aftershock of all ailments from shellshock to culture shock. Being professionally trained to heal is important, whether you're a doctor or a shaman, A druid or a spiritual professional one way or the other people need defined roles, it works for us and so it is so. The rest of the population usually have their mothers or friends to calm them down and nurture us back to health. Most psychics are only reading from the aura and subconscious echoes available to them to examine their querrents, their patients, their customer's personal energy and deepest secrets. gifts of the developed mind that anyone can develop. Don't listen to the quack that says people are born psychic, they're just prejudiced and it's an idiotic thing to say. Finding someone who is mature and experienced isn't easy believe me and if you're interested, it's like any other game, good guys finish last.

Any-who, back to aliens and the inevitable energy raising vibes the mere mention of them brings. Aliens for many people are just an excuse to abuse others. Aliens if you don't believe in them are just a figment of people's imaginations. For the most part there are other life-forms living here on Earth with us that are alien to human existence, Mutations of the human-condition, the spirit of all life forms finding a niche in our physical energies our psyche, our spirit-bodies. Psychics can see these emanations as weird "Grey" beings; Human-like in nature- but certainly not alien to any horror movies they may have seen. Unless you live in California, they will manifest as aliens as you have grown to know them, it depends on where you are and there's a reason for that. It's a weird world indeed when you begin to see people morphing into many creations before your Eyes, spider-children for example were the first species I saw myself, but I have second sight and it doesn't freak me out. Too unbelievable? Not for those who see and understand. No need for drugs it's not a losers-club, the spirit of man used to be conjoined with the animal world more than before but now it's a life less ordinary for some of us. There's no need for me to explain to true-believers, nor do I wish to bother explaining things to people who aren't ready to understand. The void of illusion isn't the right place for spiritual manifestation, the mind is. An open mind is not enough to commune with alternate life-forms. A disciplined mind is and until you find others of similar mind, you're going to be chasing a dream in an insane asylum. It's true, don't think it isn't, I just had a reading with a psychic on the edge, "Girl Interrupted" and she left the residue of the man she is Trolling behind, that's a weird world to suffer, believe me. Abuse is one path towards enlightened existence. That means normal non-drug induced spiritual development, this thing is for myself whenever I open up to certain phenomenon I need perfect calm or someone to focus my energy on otherwise its inviting outside influences from Tom, Dick and Harry in the local vicinity. That means undisciplined minds and destructive energy, so it's mentally disastrous. Having a reason to explore the realm of the subconscious and its close cousin the spirit-world is vital for mental health. Healing is the inevitable outcome whenever you realize that's what's on the cards. If you survive the usual path most people take i.e. drug-induced recreational experimentation that leads to selfish reasons for sharing gifts or healing energies. If you're character doesn't become a characteristic of the village idiot. Ever hear the expression "You may be a character but that doesn't mean you have character" The type of person born to be a healer or a spiritual revolutionary ends up most of the time becoming the worst example of humanities failures. Why? Because revolution leads to reactionary self-centered blame-ridden immature victims of self-destructive negative energy. Where the fittest survive the witless surrender. I have been lucky to see the world of spirit before my peers began to fall into chemical-induced party frenzy peer-pressured ecstasy. I gave up all vice except coffee and cigarettes and remain open to most drugs of choice because I'm not anti anything, live and let live. I'm not interested in hate or revenge but don't cross me, I am into vengeance in a big way, we have to defend ourselves and if you're interested in healing you will find reactionary forces born to destroy you.

Why do sensitive young people fall into a life of vice? For this same reason, rebellion against the drone-laden slaves of an empty society that rejects the world, the earth and the spirit-world we are all born from and all return to when our bodies die. Exiting? Yes very, what's my drug of choice? Fighting for life. Life isn't an illusion, sight is. Sight as it stands like all the senses can be explained scientifically, but here were explaining things when we can be bothered, spiritually. If there is a third eye then there's a third ear and mouth too. Where are they? Work it out for yourself? Not likely! Whatever goes on in your head when psychic phenomenon occurs can be seen with Kirlian photography along with extensive knowledge to do with reading auras. The spiritual soundwaves that take place in our heads when using clairvoyance or telekinesis can clearly be seen by the colors of aura patterns in the brain, exiting stuff eh? Yawn, but seriously, you can read thought patterns via aura and see different parts of the brain being used so obviously our brains are designed to be utilized for psychic use. Natural psychic availability that can be developed with wholesome peaceful means, no hype no histrionics, just good people using their heads for goodness and natural healing methods. The battle between good and evil goes on trying to find its way into our heads, or should I say the political struggle between opposing natural forces finds its way into our lives. Many reasons are sold down the line, much denial of facts and reason are put in the way of the same but still some good can be created during this process. Like how to deal with negative energy, we would never know how to exorcise demons if we never tried. Someone must have had the good sense to choose good to fight evil. Some decide to oppose reason and logic with their own illogical theories probably because they identify with being victims of good people and goodness. These energies are attracted to likeness, in the meantime good being constructive doesn't see evil as destructive, just necessary for the purpose of healing, an oxymoron? Probably. In the greater scheme of things opposites are an integral part of creation and without them there would be nothing but space-dust. So be careful out there, you'll need to be good if you're going to survive, in the long-term. Bluer than blue, how do you do.

The more sense you make, the harder it gets, so write with easy-breeziness and we will read between the lines, we will fill in the gaps and hear what's being said by your muse. Like many things, beating evil or such the like is usually within earshot of the dumb and stupid people. Unenlightened for a reason and for the purpose of, from a very young age of dealing with certain inherited karma. It's all good and if they become addicts to alcohol they may give it up also. Becoming an addict is good sometimes because it leads to finality. The addict decides enough is enough and tries to get clean, usually by the intersession of religious fanaticism but desperate times call for desperate measures. The supposed alien life-forms living here with us earthlings today are very susceptible to any stimulus especially when living in our bodies or mixed hybrid species. Now I'm not a big E.T. fanatic but I know that when I tap into them they prove to me that their existence is far more me than I'm letting myself realize. Only I keep them at a distance, I'm probably residual energy myself, to them and am being spoken to via time travel of a sort.

Today, in the world we live in a perplexing scenario awaits us indeed. When you're in the zone and your flying at it, it doesn't really matter and life can be high paced and energetic regardless of what age you are. When your allowing angels to bless the moment it can be helpful beyond measure. That's what I do now and I incorporate angels into my work when dealing with clients in my readings. Most people who call are spiritual and sensitive anyway and respond with love and are welcoming to angelic spirits. It's peaceful and there's plenty of energy at the same time. But it's only people who are ready to live as angels themselves that can truly keep the energy going or call on it when it's needed. Angels are in our nature, we are of the same stuff, we just forget quickly their presence around us in childhood, and nobody really invites them in again unless they're into doing so. Doing so is possible but first you'll probably have done everything you can to find sanctuary first. Faced with normal situations where commonsense is needed a mature and well-informed approach is usually the only technique. Noticing the mention of style? Style and the practice of camouflage, hiding in dark places and finding your path down through back-streets, doubling back to throw the opposition off the scent. Hiding from negative energies and their ignorant victims (poor devils)

You see, being special has its pros and cons, having the privilege of mental health and needing to work or fight to keep it in this new era where everything is needed, is a protocol. Not too much of this or not too much of the other. The inner-monologue of inner-critic and intuitive translation of our proverbial "Headspace" invaders leaves us little inner-peace to practice safe codes of conduct. The so-called collective consciousness of the masses needs constant pampering depending on where you live and what streets you choose to go down. The constant mental arithmetic and athletic maneuvers needed to avoid denting the already wounded egos of the many reactionary factions of our unwelcome mental/spiritual visitors i.e. the common man. The only defense against this raging tide of dambusting, wide-spread status-complex Imbecile-prone population is, to listen. Too easy is it to attain new heights of praise and appreciation have we when put to the test by the personalities of over-sensitive victims of the seven deadly sins. Lose yourself in the enemy's mind-frame, see what he or she sees in the school of hard knocks, or the world outside and the horror that flies by day. Figure out what they have figured out, listen to the beast made man, or woman. They have something to say about why life has sent them to this planet, why love and hurt are one and the same and ultimately why they are still human after all. Wouldn't you be safe in the knowledge that money is the route of all evil and that rules are made to be broken. Brake every rule, rich people do (supposedly) does that mean it's ok to break the moral laws or the law of nature? (Metaphorically)

Should the world of men and women not be avoided when it threatens our convictions that individual choice is a moral one. Can we not see the mask of a fool represents his master, the bank, the taxpayer, the thief? The ritual of addictive thought patterns that bring us back to blame. The big one, blame. If no-ones to blame then neither are we, me or you, or the ignorant un-educated mob, rich people, or the victims of the oppression enforced by the ignorant mob, created by the rich (Whom we forgive). If being diddled is a holistic part of life then there must be concrete reasons for it. Energy.

Energy on Earth has been riddled with change and a natural law, forever. That's a word isn't it? Forever. For forever and a day, this day, all life is ruled by cause and effect, therefore it stands to reason (another beautiful word) that energy is always moving (molecularly), or waiting to be moved or as a black hole would say if it had a gob, "I'm waiting!"

Are Black Holes the waiters of the Universe? Yes! Of course and major whatever in the meantime. There's no inevitable conclusion involved for anything especially for the uninvolved mind. Uninvolved equals unevolved. The picture of Summer is here, its July! Chill out and enjoy it for Christ's sake! Live a little, face your fears and beat the monkey on your backs for a change. Picture a beautiful young woman of about, let's say, 27, walking her young baby along a country road and enjoy the Cosmos. A green setting full of birds tweeting and a slight sway of the trees in the summer breeze. Now try to become her, weather you're male or female, it doesn't matter, or try to think that you are her Guardian Angel and only interested in her good thoughts and all that encompasses goodness, even the more serious tasks of responsibility and awareness of traffic e.t.c. How easy is it for you to do this, easy? Or a little hard to keep up your happy spirits, even almost impossible due to the negative or destructive thoughts that are clouding your mind. Getting the picture? We all that have sunny dispositions are affected sometimes by that voice we hear in our headspace. Face that voice and try to learn how to see it clearly as an uninvited unwelcome psychology from unhappy or vehemently jealous or vengeful rivals. Negative thoughts have to come from somewhere and with enough practice can be a hidden blessing resulting in financial rewards when you become a healer or therapist in the struggle for mental and spiritual health. In your defense, there's a solution. Of course we can all be affected by the weather, but only because it's easier for negative people to feed negative spirits and be used by them to utilize their unshakable need for suffering and attention.

I myself don't like suffering and have taken to using magic spells to quell the subconscious awakening of local rivals. In so doing I can bind them from attacking me and others. It works wonders on sensitive people after a lifetime of prayer has made you square and still in need. The power of Magic can defend us well especially when we can communicate directly with the spirits infecting our rivals rather than directly with their human vessels probably unable to communicate because of their hidden pain and ill-intentions(poor devils) Tools for introduction I call them, instant messages directed towards the uninitiated disciple. Ah grasshopper, its fascinating stuff indeed to keep the peasant folk at bay and free the body and soul, is it not? Making space inside and out for the higher angels of others. If an annoying person can be controlled by negative need, they too can they be affected or controlled by positive forces and with firm will on your part to do so. In the beginning of time people where a part of the whole, with divine energy and natural spiritual essences e.t.c. Although it is usually impossible to defend ourselves properly, or un attach ourselves from attached angry people. Are we now remembering our past and seeing not only the royally-dressed ancestors but also the hardly dressed beings of our true earth-connections. I stopped making sense when I started seeing the message as it shows itself. When reading for people the first message is always the last. The face that comes through visually or the messages themselves that manifest originally. Yesterday I had a woman that looked like (was) she was being controlled by natural Earth-Religion energy to keep her struggling. Until she realizes she is of earthy people who worked the land and worshipped Earth-Religion gods and goddesses she will remain broke. Start with the little people, talk to them in your mind, no one will ever know.

Realizations spring eternal growth and learning to free ourselves from being bound by the will of others. Profound it is indeed to the will of jealous eyes, ears and hearts, our countenance, but when you are free and have found your space in escape then breathing truths is food for the soul. You read books by other self-realized souls and you know they are close to you, you and you alone. For a moment they make you feel more important than them, but it's only a ploy to defend themselves ultimately from our own petty envious fear of success. If I don't try, because other people will hurt me if I do, then I should hurt successful people to prove they are weak and I am strong. Stupid thoughts make stupid people. We are weak, we are ignorant, we are a product of shallow celebrity worshipping false idols, make the rich richer and the poor poorer. Being successful isn't about vanity or proving superiority, failure is. Be successful, be a winner, use euphemisms from foreign countries you secretly want to pull a Swartzneiger on. We are all ultimately born to rule our own royal kingdom. humble or courageous, brave or stupid, life's a bia-itcha! And then she's also a supreme being! Good and bad up and down, to the right of me a joker to the left a clown. Constant echoes from our secretive minds, collective consciousness. Some superiority never sees the light of day, some sees only addiction and failure. Giving to others is balancing what's being taken away, our personal life-paths. Passion precedes panic, purity and pleasure... screamers or soothing chorus, the best of both worlds battling it out in small time manifesto, can't you see its all opera, all melodrama all representative of good and evil. Moving into another day where the sibling-nationalistic-rivalry connections we have with the sunrise of other nations squeezing some new order from our already used up life-forces. Blame game verses responsibility and responsibility verses well, ahem! Sometimes you have to let go a little. I mean our supposed addictions from the past have some connections with our true personal life-experience, even with our true calling in life. We have tried to find love in all the wrong places sometimes in every place and always wicked and wonderfully sinful! Oh yes my friend I have been good and locked up in the neighborhood of Rapunsel or hermitage with and against my will indeed, indeed, indeed. For ten long years I've struggled with my peers and pressure, with learning experiences (are there any other kind?) Pain and suffering, moaning souls of misfortune, lessons of purgatorial agonies far beyond the outer-reaches of Hell's kitchen(believe me) But along with pain came spiritual awakening, more than enough and it always seemed to precede painful experiences that lead to stress or more to the point, stress-relief (you know what I mean) This is it! This is what I've been waiting for, what you have been waiting for all your life- stress-relief that brings love and emotion and all the astral pleasures that your soul can imagine! Believe me it's a blockbuster of primordial essence exploding from your crown chakra and into an eternal land of blissful heavenly encounters. That's if you have spiritual awakening in your life, hurry up and get some! Come on the light is fading fast and nobodies on the freight-train to Nirvana! Too much wasted energy goes into suffering and guilt makes you fat (metaphorically)

Make up with your miserable doppelganger and try to balance weakness with insufferable strengths. Give peace a chance, lather yourself in ambition and believe that anything is possible. Try to plan tomorrow like when you where youthful and positive about the Zen of energizing the future even if it's only going out on the astral-plain. Anyway here we are, after years of working with anti-Christ idiotic imbeciles and all the sundry diabolical wasters you're nightmares are fuelled and driven by and yet you're still reflective and compassionate towards them. Or should I say what they represent, for all of us non-imbeciles the rest of humanity has to encompass the residual energies of all destructive universal or earthly energy. That is, all destructive people we allow access into our lives in our formative years (probably as a compromise) through our own ignorance and inexperience are given the opportunity to cease while the going is good, our dreams and personal lives, to then destroy, divide and conquer. As we begin to realize our mistakes we can clearly see that bad company is the cause of all of our failures, and more so. Leaving destructive people behind isn't impossible and can also be eternally satisfying. Before we know what's hit us, their other victims are coming to us for help, and all we can offer to save them from suicide or murder, is the attempt to escape. It's incredible and fascinating to see what escaping fascistic retribution can bring to the victims of destructive and idiotic people.

Haven't you seen it in your own life, some impoverished underprivileged victim of abuse enters your life in the guise of artistic revolutionary only to prove more pathetic than the supposed oppressors they inevitably represent? With nothing to prove, nothing to say but self-reassuring appreciation followed by the depreciation of your own identity and life-assuring self-worth. We as living breathing beings need to let in the mistakes earlier on in life to get rid of them in our middle-age and after. Forgive and let go, but never forget that learning experiences are due to the lack of leadership and properly functioning societies. If it wasn't for dope-smoking hippies some of us would never have seen the light and embraced spiritual discipline and rejected egoistic morons. Leaving moronic imbeciles behind and losing the same aspects of your own character. When you stopped ingesting the light sucking weed, of course.

The reasons you should get exited is, because when, or as soon as you realize that your failure is being caused by investing in others failures that are your self-made creations. Therefore there's know-one to blame but yourself. Ultimately subconsciously we allow our god-given enemies into our lives because we are aware of why they are there in the first-place. We know there's a plan for us and if it isn't materializing we see chance as a fine thing and let all a sundry enter with their life's plan instead of our own. We begin to see our destroyers as hired mercenaries that are a secret self-planned scheme to prove our sacrificial dream of success ultimately a ploy against god. Stop making sense and give up! Let go of fear and take hold of your destiny. Enjoy the journey in and out of poverty and or, out of destructive relationships. Wayhay! Even when at rest and a peaceful atmosphere precedes you can still be intrigued when your proper life's path revealed. Look at all the rock stars who died, because they were surrounded by enemies, jealous rivals, and that within their own bands, Jim Morrison, Janis Joplin, Elvis Presley, Amy Winehouse, there are hundreds of famous people who died because their enemies were closer to them than their friends. People without souls, should never be a part of our lives.

Trust

An order of the day is to trust and believe in selling, selling freedom to the entrapped intrepid explorer living in a metaphorical universe. An existence beyond normal expectation where no person has been before, illusion- supposedly.

Travel back in time, we all do it, in spirit, in our bending of time are we not travelling in spirit on the astral plane/ don't we actually see the past and if so cannot the people there not interact with us. It stands to reason that if future beings can imagine themselves projected back into our time to interact with us, then why not beings that apply direct energy influence i.e. you and me. That is sort of like a séance with us, except were not in spirit yet, but we are, we are in spirit just we still have our physical bodies, get it? Were here, behind the people in front of us, time wise, were thousands and millions of years behind the beings before us. Back and forth, to and fro, here and there, anything is plausible. A thousand years from now some enchanted being experiments with his spiritual powers that we invented or got wise to in this new millennium. The reality is that already things are being revealed to people that are gifted and have the luck to survive non-believers attacks on their psyche or their beliefs. Enlightenment can be transferred from one generation to another. All cultures ironically used to have enlightened beings before industrialization uprooted earthly-bound religions from the source of their power, Druids, Jews (survived the mega-attempts to annihilate them) even Christianity started off well but inevitably if you worship martyrdom you inevitably have to compromise, or like lemmings, have to jump off the nearest cliff in order to fulfill the all-important prophesy, that failure is inevitable (God forgive them) We all make compromises. If the Buddha gets in your way on the path to enlightenment-kill him. It's a metaphor! Do as I say not as I do said Christ (to pay him a compliment) Be good, be powerful, defeat the ignorant bumbling local philistines. Overcome the bully, find their disease, seek out their weakness (he or she is obsessed about finding yours.) People cannot stop but the blame for their primal fears on un-suspecting sensitive's. It's a political mine-field of the psyche of the impoverished mind. It's a pestilence on our well-bred sanctity, a cry for help all good well-educated well paid doctors or healers or publicans hear. There's money in muck!

Imbalance is unfair, greed is need, taking by force is un-natural but not to the beast that lives within, the devil inside. A creed for greedy needy dented-ego victims of karma. The short end of all sticks, the underdog. Serve the master, only if they get to pull down the middle-man. Don't mess with Mr. in-between. Ultimately they don't really want to abuse the system they just want it to work.

Anyway back to constructive people, you'll have to forgive my babbling on sometimes although it does increase the diseased interest of the insipid curiosities of local demons and their favorite vessels: brainless lobotomized troglodytes. For whom without them there would be no batteries of fuel-enhancing opportunistic mercenaries of failure and agonizing defeatist defamation. Eye on the fly. It's a hobby, it's a calling, it's a profession. Beware the doppelgangers of the apocalypse!

If it's all in the mind then listen carefully, what gets you out of bed in the morning, when you're exited about something? When was the last time you where exited about anything? Apart from millennium anxiety syndrome. When where you last connected to positive people and are you struggling to fight against negative people that annoy, control and drain you? Join the rest of the human race, 1 plus 2 equals 3: you've seen these questions before haven't you? You are human whether or not you like it. Your inner wolf or goat or cat or whatever represents your inner self is all to do with spiritual things, not evil animalistic nature. I'm used to waking up in a world gone mad, looking for some theory to get me through another day on this metaphorical world of illusion and reliance. Its insanity! Break out the strait jackets, that's life! No matter how well you apply yourself, nothing ever changes except your ability to have inner peace which coincidently occurs during the opposing apocalypse and Armageddon(every thousand years or so). That's how important the ever-changing rearranging movement of inner-peace is. Hard to grasp and easy to let go of, but essential to our existence as individuals living on the same plane or sphere of existence. What defines us as beings of higher conscience are our responsibilities outside of our own selves, not our reputations in the local vicinity, are we reasonably accepted as being good or encapsulating a grey area of pigeonhole place and name? We all have grey areas, some more than others, but only one half of us know it! Getting past the technical difficulties isn't easy and even when you're reasonably clear of foul and faceless vindictive negativity you're still going to find a positive mental attitude necessary for survival, obviously. Analyze this and you're well on your way to freedom and of course earning your stripes. Freedom, freedom is a very fine thing indeed especially when you have earned and deserve it. In this apocalyptic universal Armageddon of metaphor and reflection, all humanoid beings are possessed with the ability to understand that's going on from person to person, given the chance. Were all equipped with the same abilities and functioning sensitivities, most of us. As we make our way through the day and have the time to reflect on our lives development. Some of us are on a quest for self understanding with the sole purpose of general respect for life, and other people. seeking solutions for the crafty buggers and stressed-out mean old Wanna-beez taxing our time just to see if helping them or caring about them will get them to lay off(as long as they can also be avoided) Seeking solutions or seeking someone's else's solution, now that's an important and vital statistic. The Rabbits are in town, it's Friday night and if they can't get laid then it's time for a fight! Everybody's a Martyr everybody's a Scapegoat one way or the other, if stress doesn't lead to aggression or addiction it leads to desperation, the last act of a desperate person? Absolution!, solution. Solution, absolution or bust! At this moment where nobodies business seems to be everybody's in a world of contradictions that leads to addiction, where's the harm in chaos or harmony? Where's the harm in living by your own rules? Leaving others to chance, or even Fate? Common mistakes made in error are the call of ignorant youth or folly. Living in an environment of idiocy and constant constraint, a land that thought forgot, a cataclysmic seductive melodramatic order of chaos, falling short on dangerous hesitation. What do we do with abominable expression? With the cost of melancholy? With the order of decay, nothing? Some of us do, hear the cry for help that general mobmentalities possess, where does the psyche of illness go where humanity lies dormant. Metaphorically speaking of course, someone is at the wheel and doesn't have scruples or conscience just an awareness of cause and effect. A fairness unequalled in Heavenly grace in gods and angels where disgrace is concerned, where critiques and claims to sin or mistakes break even in our un-privileged victims of inherited crimes and creed are commonplace. Depth of character saving even the lowliest of vermin from absolute disgrace. Judging filth and scum has instant effects on you; you're involved with their low-vibration subconscious psychic telepathic temporarily possessed demonic consciousness. Looking at the pervert that's turning your stomach is letting yourself open up to the spirits involved sometimes, not all the time. Look away, look at someone nice instead, oppose it, with its opposite. You know whenever you feel some horrible repugnant vibe before you meet them it's not normal and yet its connected to some event in your future, like an interview the next day or even a week away that you're dreading but you aren't sure why. It's because of the lowest persons energy, the person that is closest to evil spirits and self-destructive energy that you're about to meet. Although depending on where you see people, who they are with and why they are forgetting that they are human. All week you're forced to accept that until this meeting or event is over your flesh will crawl and your body feels like its being manipulated and abused beyond any limitations you can accept. Horrors that all psychic or sensitive people have to experience from time to time. Unacceptable, but what if it's at the work-place, and you have to go in? What then? Take some anti-depressants? All we can hope for is that fate has thrown us a dodgy hand and if we quit or move house or whatever, we should just be ok. Hope springs eternal most of the time and when it doesn't, just grin and bear it for the moment and you will be allright, until you can escape their energy and find new circumstances. When you do get your daily inspiration, use it!

CHAPTER TWO

Percentage wise, our inspiration comes from other people, living or in spirit, actively or indirectly. Inspiration can also come from repelling the horror of non-believers sliming their way into our workspace, barren empty zombie souls seeking refuge in energy. Where do all these horror movies come from anyway? Hollywood's imaginative artistic writers or perhaps out of the quagmire of human subconsciousness. Exclusive footage into the minds of creative monster-mad scientists and ghouls, vampires and aliens, where do you draw the line, is there a line, there must be, there is, I'm sure there is, but is there. In a Universe of energy seeking new representations of itself, there can only be truth, it's impossible for any representation of abominable mutations not to exist. Diseased molecules mutating into life-forms beyond the creator gods plan for human-animal existence. So if that's the plan that encompasses some of our learning experiences, metaphysically metamorphosising right before your eyes, then where's it all going to? Who's concentrating on sanity? Where does the human being fit into in all this cosmic codswallop, high shenanigans?

Busting loose type of authorship I know, but still, the reason for it is survival. Being able to create is one way to theorize in private on the convictions I have formed myself. But in an environment that has spawned "Spawn" itself or aliens or pixies-fairies and ghosts e.t.c a creative process involving the elemental vibrations of several spiritual manifestations. For the adept believer, just a matter of tuning into it and getting used to the usual suspects. Don't feed them after midnight e.t.c. There are spirit animals or familiars in our plane of existence. They are wonderful mythic beings that manifest through the thoughts of gods and into our lives. We need to ascertain what our goals are in order to affiliate with them. Oh loosen up me why don't you? Chill with the vibe and get on board the night train. Seeing is believing but using is keeping. Unless we use our familiars regularly we lose them and their power to heal and create miracles. Also we cannot utilize our own power unless we help others in a professional capacity. Boring? Such is life, life springs eternal and some people never let boredom in, it's wonderful to choose life and be creative in work. You can play with style and technique constantly and express yourself temporarily through other people's private-personal energy.

If they want you to, of course. Knowing that other people are, just different types of energy, law of spirit is understanding the law of energy. People can change metaphysically and mutate and morph into animal forms with or without disciplined spiritual techniques. At this time we are all subjected to certain manifestations depending on our physical activity and mental influences on our spirit-bodies. I see this all the time, some people are reasonably fine until they are affected by negative forces, parents, partners or public. Strangers affect us of course especially the overly familiar ones that invite themselves into our day or space or life. Unwelcome is the world outside and the horror that roams at night. Stopped going out at night recently? Or since the first day of the new millennium, you're not alone believe me.

As a musician I'm open to gig for the public but not to fraternize with them. Musicianship is work and punters are never to be trifled with. The rarest Bible quote for me is the most important, something like "Subtlety is the power that destroys" I'm not sure if that's in the Bible but my point is that our existence is now obviously effected by subtle forces, forces beyond reality and normal existence. Paranormal alien forces that thwart our ability to see the world as it truly is or should be. Like some of us are being pulled into a void or a black hole and being ushered there by fallen angels. People who haven't realized their angelic nature has been disrupted and affected to a degree of no-return. Listen to the songs around you, watch the movies or give up media and look to the skies at sunset or sunrise and see what is so obvious to the rest of us. Signs, so its prophesized, there will be signs, there are signs, and one will is pitted against the next in a battle for supremacies. Good people have to battle ignorant people and without malice or intent. Not so easy to master the tricky trickster about your house and home or in the workplace is it? I can't take any more, isn't the last thing I have ever said and I hope it won't be yours. You bought the book, you deal with it. Your Mother is possessed by the Divil? Deal with it, your Father is the Divil! Same problem, deal with it, pull out your hair, scream and yell "What's happening to me!"get a divorce, or a new job, or any job you can survive in, hide from the world, from your old friends and enemies, the end is nigh! Run! Run for your lives!

What is this madman baulking on about? Not you fool, not you. It's always somebody else's problem, isn't it? You've never really had to deal with suicidal thoughts or depression until now. You could always handle life, one way or the other? Usually, but things have changed over the last few years, haven't they? They will, grasshopper, one day soon, and if you're lucky you'll recover in time to save your own life! I did, and only just, I made my own luck. Now I'm helping other people survive the near evil imbeciles that karma, that cruel mother, spoils their lives with. Meer strangers that lead you on to horrors infinite revenge. Getting justice on negative people is sometimes on your mind and murder not far from your tongue. That's good! You're letting it all out, getting rid of frustration and seething at the agonizing perils before you. Plunging into an abyss of bottomless pressurizing sexual advances from ugly and repulsive dirty repugnant abusive moronic imbeciles. They used to be human but now they have mutated into something more un-natural. As it seems more than possible, paranormal mutations, the other people in your life sometimes are released from this evil serpent-demon and allowed to seek justice for being blamed by you for having to suffer their possessed state. You saw their situation and suffered their wrath and now that they are temporarily free from its grip because of god knows what reason, (Christmas) or whatever, their back in your life, on your astral plane and hunting for blame. How dare you see me in a bad light, they say, were beautiful, were special, you're alone. You're not alone, they're just making you feel like you are. The same spirit that possesses them (intermittingly) usually has granted some temporary reprieve and when they're released it sends them you're way. Look around and ask, "Show me" to your spirit-guides, they will reveal the specter responsible. Unusual activity, doesn't have to be negative, its can also be uplifting, as it should be, or will be more so as you progress in degrees of experience and adepthood.

It's not all doom and gloom, and where many have hung themselves because of stress, fear, ignorance, panic, guilt or whatever, you will survive. You will fight like a god and scream your head off and curse the screaming haunting poltergeist amadans outside your bedroom window, or hovering over your head.

Roll wind roll, upon the head of the lion, I will walk on the head of the worm. I will scream at the screamers and sell out their lies till death comes for me and all the victims and hypocrites and anti-Christ's. Dramatic isn't it? As a spiritual person I get it all the time, as well most of you will too, so never say die, let the demons see they are seen in the bodies of our unwelcome visitors. Names and places of harassing people can be seen via remote viewing. Be careful not to attack people, they know not what they do. They will haunt you for twenty years before you come up with a solution for their haunting of you. Seek help now, study reiki! Angels, light working, experiment with spiritualists wherever you can.

Angry spirits, restless spirits, in the bodies of idiots. Basically they are sure that your to blame for everything, you're evil and they are good. That you're everything they are being told you are by the voices that rule them, and will scream it at you astrally for the rest of your life, if you let them. Why? Because they are stupid (intermittingly) or ignorant, or blind, deaf and dumb, you're to blame for all the evil in the world, if they want you to be, they're not delusional, they're just listening to the Divils little helpers, the voice of suspicion. It's all on now, isn't it people, and the buck stops at experience. Or buy a canopy for your bed.

Living in a world bent on educating the next generation is one thing, ceasing to be the next generation is another. Becoming the ultimate substitute for humanities last great hope is now the responsibility of our elders because many of our youth or our peers are failing to reach the requirements for global representatives. Politicians aren't spiritual people and religious people aren't open-minded enough for the new order of things. Basically the new age has failed in many ways to reach its full potential because we have emphasized with material needs instead of spiritual ones. Even the spiritual revolution made rich people richer and tarot reading psychic mediums just barely survive. Oh what would life be if we were a little greedier and a lot more scrupulous, a short road to Hell that's what.

Look, a few months ago I changed my life a whole lot by seeking work as a medium again and I knew it would lead to chasing rainbows and believing in impossible dreams. Even though I am now doing well. Sure enough we all need to suffer for a cause and a good cause, but I know when my goose really is cooked sometimes. There's no use in flogging a dead horse when it comes to marriage and normality, that's life, I'm a non-drinking alcoholic because I never joined the pioneers, a religious fanatic because I don't bend and take grief from monsters(Metaphorically and physically) a non-believer for keeping my head screwed on right and a loser for leaving the world behind. Even the suicide club rejects my status as non-dead messiah! Life's a bewitcha-sucker! And that's the truth! It stinks, it smells and it shoves perverted poltergeistic scum from Hell in your face just for starters. Get used to it, otherwise you're going to be the one that recruits teenagers for the next generation of gender benders pimp-prostitutes and their favorite politicians as they reduce the age of consent to even lower levels. Cop on to yourself and realize that you're the victim of peer-pressure and everybody's copping out for their favorite class-addiction, drugs, drink and sexual dysfunction. What the Hell is going on! And how much does it cost. My books, worse case scenario, entertainment only, must be over 18.

How much time do we have, where are we going and what's all this were all about? Usually I'm cocooned in an inner world of wisdom worshipping, hiding from the incessant infidel hoards when suddenly it's New Years Eve! People are opening up to positivity just on the day itself, like it's safe to do so. Bundle up your fears and let them fly away for all they're worth! A new year thank God! We've beaten the Devil (No more Divils)for another year and it really feels like it doesn't it? Remember to let old acquaintances go, water under the bridge. Goodness exists and it's for us the happy fools throwing caution to the wind once again Wayhay"! Even though I'm like this every day, a happy spa, that's me.

New Years Eve is tomorrow and I can always feel the hopefulness that really decent people bring into their lives, for their children's futures, it's a truly magnificent victory over the past, a real blessing. What would life be like if we could all muster up some courage and face our futures with love. It's not so hard to do if you're lucky and you apply yourself. Sure some of us need drugs to help fight stress and tension, but that's ok. The world is built on feelings and sensitivities. Breath, feel your heart beat, that's you, yknow?

Now that I've got your attention, something has mine. Its opposing our position on the positive, could it be that something good is about to happen, yknow? When you've become numb to the lingering doubts around and decided that numbness is officially the newest craze in your life? At last, you've been pushed too far or so far that eventually surrender to opposing forces has taken its toll. All those years of being a positive constructive person has failed to save your demeanor. Past the point of no return if only for an instant...I can't go on, my back is bent, my feet are sore, my knees are weak "Oh Hell God! Take me now".

Its hard work being good, it doesn't help to become devoted to God and then splurge out just because you need the comfort of the things your avoiding, you're a "Yo-Yo" Sin-abstinence-sin-abstinence, your body eventually starts breaking down along with the rest of your life. Lazarus complex is what we call it, fly high like an eagle, then fall down into the pleasures of the flesh, even after desperately trying not to, you give in to temptation around Thursday, or during the fool Moon, like every other healer the world round. Karma-penitence-spiritual high-stress-temptation-failure-sin-pleasure (Sex-of some sort) you have to give in at some stage, because everybody else does and that collective giving in is what beats you. You wanna be a nun, go live in a nunnery and see what that's like. Ask an Anglican Priest when was the last time he relived himself, probably never, he has a wife for that Wednesday evening session, ask a Catholic priest, he wont tell you, but its probably more than just once a week, not very spiritual, or fair eh?

Now you're ready for some therapy, directly, to the body. Massage or a new mattress, possibly some celibacy to rejuvenate your body and soul. Some reformation that vexes your enemies and delivers unto you your path, the quest for success-riches beyond your wildest dreams! Oh boy! I can't wait for that one, but first we must become rich within. Baby you're a rich man! Woman! Or amoeba! Temporarily until the inevitable "Yo-Yo" effect repeats itself, again, and again, and again, at this stage you're a professional "Astral" Casanova/Gandhi/Messiah! Or tight wearing Buddhist monk.

Deep down inside the struggle continues and your audience apart from being enraptured by the Muse is free of inhibitive contradictions. Stop making sense, drive the critics away, give way to that power you've got rumbling inside and create! Rising tides give sway to lives extraordinary, lives of passion and success. More to the point, let's have some sanity around here and do a little work. Create! Bang crash wallop! Get moving, quickly, pick up a drum and bang it, stomp your feet, kill the demented! (Pardon my Fringlish) Jump, shout, let it all out. Get moving, keep going, like when you were a child, run for god's sake run! Shed those extra pounds you're holding onto ever since you've had your last baby, man! This is the time of equality, where nerds can be famous and rule, fat is the new thin, Ugly the new "Special" Kiss my white ego! Kiss my big white supraconsciousness! Utopia rules! T.V. is the Truth, there is hope that all failures are one big mess of possible consumer product and "Potential" for the rich to get richer, join in the fun!

There has to be an out for those who do. For those of us that can, make a difference, to other people's lives. You write a song, you find a musician, or two (with half a brain between them) and you do your first gig! Great! You're on the road, doing gigs. Before you know it, you're on the radio, a little, maybe even a T.V. appearance just for laughs. Even though it's only a showcase for new talent, you think for one second that it's going to last then boom, its over. It's all over and you feel like killing yourself, or maybe the other band members. We could have been huge! We made it into Hotpress Magazine, people where talking about us making it, but failure raised its ugly white bread head, why? One hundred thousand reasons why losers choose to lose, they identify with failure, destroying your dreams and theirs. In one foul stroke: it's over.

Back up on the horse buddy, or it really is over. Get back up there quick, back to creating somehow, something, rapido! Orifice painting, anything, It aint easy, but then, it's also never been easier. I have just helped my friend get work with an American company called (Blank of the blank). Magnificant! Absolutely wonderful, also working for (Blank the blank) which is very helpful, although sometimes you're fighting non-believers constantly, other psychics who can't understand their role in society, or get up the gumption to finally start working as a professional, non-believers. Anti-Christ's armed with tweed jackets, cowhide handbags and rosary beads. Also working for one site that serves four other sites altogether, including two internationally famous spirit mediums whos faces front the site as their personal site (not) (One which is now in spirit himself).

It's great to tune into friendly people and allow them to listen to their own Angels. High speed Locomotives cannot and should not be slowed down instantly, it's a waste of energy. If something is meant to be, it will happen gently and without too much effort, with a little help from your good friend experience of course. Keeping your head when most needed is vital, of course where knowledge is more easily applied. The power of Light! Can lift you up to higher planes. When the goings good, dance. Ever thought of yourself as a high-flyer, well believe it or not it does take determination and effort. Effort and willpower, not the stressed-out determination, although it can be stressful because of other people and or accidents of nature. Keeping the ball rolling through thick and thin, year in, year out isn't easy for many reasons.

You may be obsessed by reason, logically. Reasons to be cheerful? Tearful? Hear your fill, said your fill e.t.c. were not all teenagers lost in the limbo of other people's dreams. Some of you will be hindered until your dreams are clouded by nightmares, daycares and all asundry connected. When you've lost all your fair-weather friends and you feel it's the end, it could well be. Never stop moving. Motto one. Never stop moaning, I have literally moaned my way through twenty years of moaners. Where fire beats fire, firewall yourself from the complainers that never ever give up! You will wake up to reality some day. When life-connections gone wrong account for your failures, you may never be to blame for all the disaster. It can be accounted for by the idiots you invited into your life! Why were they invited in? To be of assistance when the alternative isn't negotiable. For instance you're living in a defeatist society where people are controlled by expectations granted to them by surrounding consciousness. Too deep? By other idiotic controlling small minded local influences i.e. school teachers from disintegrated social climates i.e. ex-colonized countries. Along came the Romans and disfunctionality in the aftermath was for ever more.

Anyone can see, I'm stuck on stupidity myself and am finding it hard to get off the subject. I do find it hard; it's like as soon as I start writing I'm surrounded by my critics. But, Ce La Vie, that's me. Also don't forget, we all have our demons to deliver, one way or the other. So I have started self-hypnosis to help get me off the subject of Hell is other people. On the good side of life, another recompense for proliferation, Genocidal efficiency (Only Joking) but seriously, where are we going? Plus its my job to work on the root causes of things and neurosis is the publics favorite drug of choice i.e. adrenaline.

I have found a path through thick and thin and have barely survived the curses placed upon me by long-suffering souls. Their pain and misery has taught them one thing, walk a mile in their shoes and see, what becomes of a man that's been outcast by his people. Thrown out into the dirt of a murderous master and forced to live like an animal. These are the ghosts of my past, the moaning damned souls of Purgatory, bodies bent double in humiliating servitude for some sort of penance. A people sent out into a cursed famine ridden hole to scrape a living from a parched bog where little food can grow and not a free soul in sight. I used to complain about moaners until I saw their souls released form a peasant lifestyle. Who cares who was the cause of such a horrific existence. The Famine was a blessing for many that were secretly praying for death anyway. What spiritual power was behind this four hundred years of humiliation and agonizing pestilence. Spat upon, made to bend down before all asundry and suffer insult and injury. To beat the humanity out of a race and them turn them against each other. To force them to live like dogs or rats and live in squalor, addicted to poteen (Moonshine). The mind of a country needs time to recover, to gain its ego back. Worse forces take over, fascistic nationalism. Change must come through the barrel of a gun. Who are these poteen ghosts and what's their message. Life is for suffering is their message. Life is suffering and like a broken record their children repeat during life that indeed, causing suffering is their life's work! Congratulations! You have just revealed the meaning of life, repelling suffering as much as possible, especially the forces behind it. The reasons for suffering, human frailty. We no longer have to live like dogs but that doesn't mean were not open to the world consciousness of experimentation after a thousand years of enforced religious doctrine. It gets worse before it gets better. There's money in muck. If the rich control the fashion forced upon the world then they control what sells, sex, more to the point sex and spirituality. After all addiction comes naturally to the sheep. The dream of success sells also. Selling pipedreams to the world sells. Telling people what to do with their lives sells. Cell phones are just one aspect of developing our ability to connect to the world, other people. Cars project a feeling of freedom for those who can afford them, and who couldn't on hire purchase! Cars also insult those who cannot afford them. But are you insulted by success? Are you insulted by Gandhi? By spiritual success? Are you cosmically obsessed about other people's supposed failure, is that your success story, other peoples failure? Who do we vote for and why is it really so important… What species, what gods, what countries do we endorse e.t.c. There is a world out there and yes even now it's waiting for you to come on through and believe in yourself, even though it's hard to do. Anything worth doing is hard. Writing this book is a success against the energy that's trying to stop it being written. I forget the failure and I inspire creativity with every day and all energy that can be lived, that represents life!

CHAPTER THREE

Now this book here that I'm writing now, apart from not giving up on romantic views is indeed supposed to be a development in my life as a writer, not as a psychic. We can leave the world behind as a shooter, moving up if we can against the flow of water in an excited mass, or comply with the flow itself. Boom! Bam! Whenever we get excited about something it's inevitable that there's a fall afterward. The energies involved in accumulating positive energy have to be phenomenally larger than the forces of mundane existence. Awesome Dude! Positively. Living in the real world means finding things we have been searching for, mostly by chance. It's the same in nature, we hunt, we find, by prayer or magic, or by chance. Living our lives and passing the time however we see fit. Running out of steam? Great, that means they're wearing you down and you're employed by the effects of apathy and general dismissal of intelligent energizing life-forces. You've got them just where you want them, believing in your tired stressed-out adherence to the same forces that have always had their number. When you get home in the evenings or after your lunchtime munch, there it is, drained tired energy calling for reinforced ends to everything. People call me all the time wondering when anything is ever going to change. Then I know that the end is near and boredoms sinking in, tired, bored, empty, wasted, apathetic, drained, negative energy sucking my positivity. Oh what's the point? Why go on? You have to sit and allow gravity to slowly pull you down, down, down. This is usually the moment I get up and take off all my clothes (Except for underwear) and say Universe, I will not stand for this! Put on my wetsuit and go for a swim or just exercise. Last week I actually put my wetsuit on but felt the people outside were too short on positivity, playing mindgames and sucking life-force, so I worked out in it! Soooo crazy. And yet I found clarity behind this new found reason. I spoke out to them and told them I wouldn't put up with their situation, (I was avoiding what I felt would be the cause of some calamity or other) and neither should they. They are only vessels for neurotic spiritual energy, or negative spirits anyway. They can't help but become affected by other peoples place outside in the world. They can be seen by all passers by and are out in all weather, hung over or not. What about all the people inside, what's their world like and what spirits affect them, day and night-night and day. The same spirits in different ways. Challenging, isn't it.

It's all happening now, the revelations that this time has promised. All the reasons behind everything is becoming clearer and clearer. I have seen in recent weeks developments in understanding in my clients for issues pertaining to their situations. Who is affecting them and how close that person is to losing their soul energy, or their physical health, or their mental health. Why positive thoughts sent out to problem causers helps understand that they are in fact in need and negative energy is helping them get attention by flagging at the world around them. The more sensitive person is rapidly affected by the part possessed soul of indiciplined mental weakness. A good countenance is necessary for a good healthy body and soul. We can help fools, where we can.

Delusive and addictive, much like the unobtrusive adherence to cohesion. Obligatory pugilistic inherent connectivity's exhibitionism. My muse? Absolutely. Are we being brainwashed? Of course we are, but depending on by whom and by what, we have alternatives. Angry destructive spirits, like the spirit of my landlords ghost that woke me up last night whilst the police were banging on the door because my water fossett was making a splash-pool of the kitchen floor.

Yes it's true, and yet I've heard this tapping before, a banging on the cottage door. The magic just happens. Legendary revelations reveal themselves whilst all asunder lose their laundry. What are you listening to, where's your head at, is your heart on the ball, on its game e.t.c.

The answer my friends is keeping busy, especially when napping, relaxing and unwinding. Thinking leads to wondering and daydreamers must inevitably learn that suffering leads to success! Don't forget, breathing leads to freedom. Four weeks later and I have realized my time in Galway is over, its too cold this winter and I managed to leave my hell bedsit for a nice granny flat in a well to do area and after three weeks there have decided to leg it outta here.

Back to my exciting life. I have just emigrated to Malta and am here, really here in this warm place, warm air, warm energy. Sounds good, but I have to find a place to live immediately if I'm to hold on to my job on the phone. Don't want to worry about mundane things and am going with the flow, trust your instincts e.t.c. feels good, following your nose and your instincts for a change, not knowing what's next apart from messages from the spirit. Hotels facing the sea and its crashing down on the rocks outside constantly. Enough sometimes is enough. So, when is enough not enough? When you become interested in money. It takes us a down a slippery slope or as we begin to see the light, it takes us upwards towards an inevitable conclusion. That's where the gold lies (Pun) The golden key to success lies in a revelation as to where the power lies, who has it, how close their telepathic awareness is to ours and why. We all veer near telepathic experiences throughout our lives, if we are living breathing human beings. We all know when there is a presence of another around us, but can we remember the first time that we felt the presence of someone because of our thoughts alone. We think of money and sometimes we attract the presence of someone connected to money, why? To explain it simply, because that's what happens. Because because. The real reasons behind everything don't matter at first, our subconscious knows them all. We attract the telepathic abilities in people who normally don't have any and if they are older than us, which most of the time they are, then they will generally choose to dominate us, naturally by their free will and association with the powers of their mental capacity, being inferior, gives them a reason to be defensive and attack. They usually become open to our analytical minds and are temporarily hyper sensitive to insulting thoughts about them. Their mind is restricted by forces, spirits, energies hundreds of thousands of years old, millennia, right here in the microcosm of your life. They associate with supposed superior energies but they still work for the man, whomsoever he may be, their boss, or their dark angel spirit guides or devils their subconscious mind generates. Fear and greed.

Why? Because, because if we gain bigger financial gain, we attract knowledge and knowledge is a powerful thing, it's also free. No charge. Free service! Knowledge. The whole time I'm writing this the presence of dark forces are all around me trying to get in. Why? Because greed is the devil and all gold belongs to him. All that glamour's and glitters, all that rules the hearts and minds of men, supposedly. But what of men and women, what of a new age designed to free us of restricting ignorance that too can only be if darkness rules first. Goodness would never allow destructive forces to battle over equality. Also, as the new age mystic/prophet I'm pertaining to be, I'm attracting beings that force information upon me. In Malta there is a large presence of the need for money from some people. I have seen what that does to ordinary people, it makes them destructively greedy. Like landladies and landlords in Ireland charging impossible prices for small accommodations. Ireland, land of the ex-easygoing, now land of expense, greed and cost, charges, foreign companies taking tax cuts as they build office blocks on ancient monuments at their ease.

Only money can give people a reason to fight or die for human rights. Suffragettes committing suicide for money, money is power. Power gives freedom to choose, even to choose life or death for you and me while were still in the womb. Why? Because of a greater evil, slavery and servitude. Those who serve mostly are forced to step over others just to survive. Minimum wage jobs leading to non-progression communities stuck in the ditches of mistake and addiction to alcohol, Nicotine, sex and the only power available to them, oppression. Controlling the people is easy if you're rich and well respected, moaning about the rich is easy if you're a bum addicted to hashish and alcohol and sex(not every day with yourself, that's just sad).

The beasts we make of ourselves because of an anachronised system, like all systems we have come up with that ultimately are designed by men who have no knowledge of humanitarian capability. Trial and error is just not good enough, yet we are all forced to live this way, constantly learning like children about pitfalls and potholes. Adjusting slowly but surely like an animal to our environment. Meanwhile, we don't have all the money and the power that we think we need, or would like to have just to see if it would make a difference, well of course it would. Big wheels keep on turning and as we speak there are forces at work around us. If you want to rise up the ladder, you first must move. house and home to a place of wealth and riches, either metaphysically or physically. For those that have enough, and just enough, that's all fine and true, but they are holding the rest of us back that need more than "Live horse, eat grass" Their mental energy is strong because they resign themselves to it and have very clear convictions towards having enough. God has put them where they are, and it true, he has, he has put you where you are too. We pray to God or gods and when they listen, we receive enough to live and eat and pay our bills.

Then our creative energies need more, we don't want to be held back by our neighbors constant jealousies and intervention, their playing god with our lives, who gave them permission, why are they so loud? Are they hiding something from the world? Who cares, well now we have to, to take a slight interest in neighbors or people who interconnect with our personal space and vibration. It's like their constantly searching for our thoughts to stop us from progressing, just because they can, and they can. Different mental paths for people who are easily led, they will do anything and all for the means of an end, just to hide from their dreams by cancelling ours, that's fear.

Now, how to escape to the other side, the side of success, without having to spend years writing books and waiting for a publishing contract, years of books, paintings, songs and still no success. Some people have had to sell their souls or make a deal with the Divil just to make it happen. Many if not most of the famous people you know have actually made a deal with Lucifer for their lifelong fame. One way or the other, they lose their soul along the way, contract or no.

Look at many of the stars of Hollywood or of the rock scene. How for so many years have they survived intact, through hell and high water to still be on top. The Stones, Bob Dylan e.t.c. all make pacts with the Divil for fame, God knows who else (Pun).

So all this talk of jealousy, peoples energies are full of fears, that's why! Jealousy holds us back. Our friends and family, our peers, our enemies, they all want to be the centre of attention. It's human nature. Deals galore…don't worry it's all in the small print, you'll see. Here and now wherever you are, remember it's in our nature to survive against all odds throughout our lives and believe it or not, rivalry is part and parcel of our existence. You'll see.

Competitiveness is pushed upon some people when they're young, whereas the rest of us are left on the sidelines watching. Then for some reason we apply ourselves, when the time is right. Holistically co-existing with minorities and majorities. Political expressionism leads to Communism and emptiness, a void of art. The energies affecting us now for example are empty, modern music has eventually caught up with the cliché of meaninglessness and people who complain are attacked as being non-conformist. It's a joke really, this new world with all its constricting anachronisms, I feel like I'm squeezing blood from a stone trying to find something of worth in it all. Just the day that's in it I suppose, the best of times, the worst of times. Life gives us a road, we usually take it, when were younger, free of fear, free of restrictions. Older and wiser helps and some adventures still abound. Here in Malta, my present abode, yes I've moved out of retarded bedsitter Hell and have seen the light of 2012 around the corner. There is a sense of peace here because of the weather I suppose. The Celtic Goddess Temples waiting forever for us Christians to make it back to the fold.

Our contemporary cave dwellers awaiting redemption from a modern world. The world has always been a tough place, it's easier in youth because were protected and don't forget, innocent. The greatest weapon against suffering is innocence. You will find being middleclass and reading this book that you may suffer at times in life, when you do, it's because of jealousies and fears, other peoples, it breeds ignorance.

Generally. Bastardised compensation for being weak in character and vain, the ego of an idiot is pure ignorance. Ignorance breeds fascism and fundamentalism, it has its drones with their same personal grudges and sameness not unlike robots or metaphors for slavery and blame. Drink is the opiate of the bored and the ignorant. If you leave school and avoid college because it's a capitalist venture set to brainwash and control, take the red pill, but be warned, living on the dole just so you can chill leads to suffering, addiction and becoming friends with your greatest of future enemies, losers, beware osmosis. Avoid college at a young age, go see a bit of the world, but don't smoke skunk weed or your finished, try moderation, try some homegrown.

Then go square, get a job and see, no more bedsits, no more horrific experiences, it's almost like a computer programme has taken over your life and freed you from the slavery of the dammed. Given the power of feeding the system and maybe even paying some tax, you will be energizing the machine, the same machine that gave you a place in the world in the first place, to a degree. People that are too hard on themselves are stressed and they will make you fail, it's their way of experiencing life, the hard way, the school outside, the poor man's university.

Their heroes are ultimate losers, famous people. Successful people that inevitably fail. Proof to them that they have the world all sussed out and need to keep the rest of us in our place. They vote for the other team, avoid at all costs the imbecile that poverty generates. Become all they despise and you will be happy, contented that life is about just this. Be good and good things will happen. Work, be charitable to the poor and they will lay off a little, be less begrudging, less verbal, less present in your life, they have it hard, they are products of pain and suffering. Forgive their oppressors, their rivals, i.e. their own siblings and peers. Make your escape, humorous or not, all of us are equal.

Those who have, have worked and suffered to get it, before you have anything, you too must suffer to make it happen. Your life has been about learning not being, its other people that are the hard work, and the other side, the good people, they are the pay off, they have suffered negative idiots too. Remind them that you are good, never fail them, always be strong. You see, knowing that a life less ordinary is going to be yours, makes it harder to get on with others a lot of the time. There's always going to be life lessons going on. There's always the need to succeed, after all your work you need to have some success, one way or the other. The Zen of success can mean being a working musician or psychic and also having to work in a supermarket, eventually life will push you into a reasonably cool place, say a nightclub where you're the D.J. or even the ticket collector. Depending on your abilities and skill. Some people place importance in their jobs that is beyond the normal, being a ticket collector isn't a very important job, but for anal people, they place importance on it. They decide to become aware of their importance and our need to be. They are gifted by lowly spirits and we are gifted by more constructive, more productive ones. The problem is, we are innocent and they are not. They are reactionary and we are normal, functioning people, but action prone. Normal has to put up with bullying sensitive's, people who try to take advantage for selfish gain. They are and will always be, waiting in the woodwork for opportunity. Be aware of them, they can be useful for many reasons; they like drama and seek it out everywhere. They are resourceful and utilize the people around them as if they are hired to do so. Eventually we all meet our true nemesis, just not in every person we meet, that's attracting paranoid thoughts, not paranoia.

Here is an island where you can, if you're very, very, careful, get to sheppard those curious minds of your nemesis', the infidel frenemies you call your local ignorant idiots, fools, losers, the general public at large, your enemies or friends, foreign devils with backwards ways of thinking, idiotic older people, absolutely idiotic younger morons and idiots, God bless em!. This blissful encounter if a personification of selfless oppression and idiocy, to the best intensions, of course. An enigma of operatic proportions beset upon the world and its children by bankers, politicians, teachers, doctors, nurses, priests and nuns, lecturers, celebrities, drug pushers, thieves and murderers(bankers e.t.c.)

Some playful trickster idiocy, the kind that we all love so well. This time its manifesting through, collective consciousness, anybody that passes by, I have been followed by the god of idiocy! The Gods representation on the island, and any other country I have been, here today, it doesn't look to friendly, but I think He will slowly see, I am a worthy project and not some local total imbecile ready to serve his darker path. Although there is good in the general population, this revelation is because of recent developments in Local microcosmic representations of my own spiritual path into asexual celibate disciplines. I have being making love on the astral plane, (through poetry only of course)of course, don't let the nerd thoughts disrupt you. Keep them out of your head. As I speak to you, reader, keep your centre, don't think while you read, it's very disturbing. If you are a psychic, you will see a female holding her jaw and apparently making a face. Just now the phone rang and the querrent was effectively the muse of this sentence. The woman holding her jaw was still manifesting whilst I read the cards, so I entered her head and could see it was a "Crones" energy using her. The emphasis was on the Woman I was talking to which happened to be a Shamanic preacher. But like all Human beings was being affected by other people, how unique (sic) How absolutely normal, talk about the same old same old, but with the theme of this day in mind, the Gods where watching. The language of lunacy, describing simple things in a clouded way, a Labyrinth of emotional and mental possibilities that can lead to Insanity, self afflicted. If weird personalities do not lead into insanity, it's because the mental person in question is just acting out, looking for release and relief by acting mad, without the aid of hashish or alcohol e.t.c. over long periods of time. The voice of reason is your conscience telling you, in mental verbal words, act sane and people will not see your inner turmoil. Otherwise it's possible; you may tread the path of people who talk to their invisible friends aloud in public in an aggressive and threatening way. Not good.

Tenet, I think is the spirit with me today, and on a small Mediterranean Island like Malta, it's no worry to realize he (The Divil or Trickster) is a manifestation of a local "out there" energy that in itself manifests in local people in the drop of a hat. Being Irish, I see this all the time when people pretend to be a local when they meet, "Howya boyo!" e.t.c. acting like Peasants from a Father Ted episode, not being able to keep it sane for even a second. Hiding their hatred and fear of each other behind false friendliness.

I was supposed to go visit the main temple today but, I felt like I wasn't meant to(I found out later when I arrived home early that it was a very busy day on the phone, so in future whenever it gets weird out there, just go home). The energy of the people was too tourist orientated, driving forces keeping me away from becoming a tourist myself. Looking for the best and the brightest Stonehenge of the lot. So I ended up realizing that a Goddess Temple was in fact right up the road from me. It can't be seen from the road and isn't accessible to the public. But there you have it, why this conflicted energy is so close to us here in St Julian's by the sea. Everybody thinks they're individuals but were all just alternate energy affected by the same rules, the same controlling sibling drives, controlled in turn by spirits of life force, saints or gods. Cats and dogs.

If our siblings have developed the gift of mental interference, control then so too the mother, grandmothers e.t.c. of neighbors, the sound of their voice becomes a controlling mechanism that creates fight or flight reactions in us, the receiver of their energy. We feel it in our stomachs, our solar plexus, Boom! Yet we can communicate via our clairvoyant "Imaginations", our mental telepathy and ensure a m more subtle approach to friendlier communication. Sending out loving and supportive vibes to all, its magic! It works on most people and it's a normal part of our lives always has been.

Revelations that to the non-believer cannot yet agree with, you should see them to your left, manifesting through any local predecessor of their ancestral D.N.A. waning down the drain. Their becoming one with the Gods of controlling emotional energy. You can all see what I'm talking about, just for most of you, it's in your subconscious. The spirits behind all of this aren't too worried, they already know what I'm talking about and for most of you, are controlling your every thought, move and deed (Action). Since childhood, positive and negative energies have introduced the personification of justice in both houses of earthly karma. I have to reinforce the paths of destiny because my last caller was wound up the hill big-time and is probably calling up to complain about me, but to no avail, anymore. The companies I work for have told me that they won't fire me if people complain, truth is they are psychic also and know what were up against here. They only care that I don't break the law and do my job.

Just because of one damned fool, the world of mental health will be oblivious to them. You do get "Karma callers" once and a while, with tricks up their sleeves, its part and parcel of the game, surviving the divil and its beasts, wherever his minions rush in to surprise you. The odd prostitute, crack addict that calls first thing on a Monday mourning to check and see if your activities merit punishment, are you on the ball? Ask yourself this question, why does it get weird, every time you slip up and have a little fun? Karma!

Still the theme of this days readings is truthful contact with the forces that be and their effects on our lives. One-sidedness is for the ignorant, however intelligent they may be. We can all fall short of the mark when it comes to our personal philosophies, over time allowing for some flexibility to manifest. Don't we. Otherwise we become neurotic, like the last caller, her energy was all over the place, stirring up a magic of destruction and death. Midway through the reading she started to criticize my attitude saying that I didn't sound happy, meanwhile her energy started attacking me and almost exploding with neurotic dizziness. I understand that from experience I was feeling what she was feeling and my spirit-guides where protecting me by making her feel dizzy. In turn she was offended by this power and became even more defensive. Whew! By the time she hung up and I wrote this, another person called with a high voltage energy also and I am sure they were connected (punishment karma)because she was a speed freak also. High, high mad energies, desperate to invoke destruction and ruin. On the phone and face to face. So, who did we offend to deserve such disastrous energies, and will we survive the week/year/decade/millennia? Who knows. Don't bother getting psychic medium insurance for home readings, get sexual harassment insurance and a damn good video surveillance system to protect yourselves from false accusations. Their solicitor will run for the hills when he knows you have clear video footage of your crack addict client entering and leaving your home, the reading itself and any rooms they may use whilst in your place of work. Murphy's law.

The aftermath of such destructive forces always leads to suffering and death, and/or death of soul and quality of life. Death of cause and effect. The metaphorical end of suffering albeit. If your disciplined enough to face your fears, sometimes fear becomes a necessity to your day, and addictive as it may seem, the cause of all your sorrow. For whom the bell tolls, some of us well know. We cause our own suffering, given time, we stop it in its tracks.

Don't panic. Motto of the day. When all around you are attacking, remember, Lemmings need protection (pun)

Not a day, everyday for letting studies stray. Behold the diagram your searching for, don't slump, that's life. Forethoughts reverbs, heard about the…anywhoo…What's the point, sometimes it's the same ol same ol rollocks, (Pardon my French) Demons threatening to destroy everything, it's like an episode of The Charmed Ones. Percy French, rollocks and pish, piffle and hogwash, balderdash, why am I wasting your time as an self important spoiled ignorant consumer anyway? Reading this crap and analyzing it continuously with your inferior brain! "I can do better" attitude. Sure, bore us all to death why don't you.

Forgive my little outburst but you can't blame me, after all I am waiting for humanity (Sunday drivers) to catch up with me and yes they have been swarming backwards recently, haven't they? Passing by your door with a self-important "You serve"! Vibration. That's my job! To serve! Servant of God, burnt at the stake for my last mistake, eaten by vultures and sold for a penny. Out of some foreign demons servants slave, begging for mercy fresh from the grave. Beggars are we, selling ourselves, rock of ages, look me up in the yellow pages. Masters of the spirit, godlike mortals filling our bellies with the fat of the land. Grief councilors in mortal combat with each other, revelations with a bang!

Deep down inside, we all secretly want this to be the last time, then when were feeling better, can't wait for the next life. I heard a man say once, "Next life" he meant that we will get it right next time round. Forget this lifetime; the grass is always greener... A good sense of humor, the last bastion of good guys. Of course, the wisdom from a fool, in this case, is no good to him, after living a life that caused more suffering than his last one, his next life, a sanctuary, will not be.

Get it right this time, or else!. 20 whatever is on the way, I wonder sometimes why we weren't aware of this before the Millennium? 1999 was the big, "This is it!" Bollonie. Ever wonder why, as a child, you never thought about the year 2000? I even used to read a comic called 2000AD. But it never awoke my awareness to the idea, even when people started talking about the Millennium, they still never mentioned 2000, it was always 1999! 1999! Like we were being stopped by some controlling force. Its like when someone breaks the record for the fasted mile, until then knowbody can even imagine what it feels like to be there, never mind breaking the record themselves. You're probably reading this in 2025 or 2060 or God knows what! Back in time?

So, collectively, we think alike, we are controlled naturally by mass consciousness, naturally. No conspiracies, just osmosis of information. A bit of both maybe, illusions adding towards possibilities, much like divination. Chance levied by possibility. Reality, smoother than fiction. Stealth is key.

Starting a new book is always, given time, a slow process for anybody. Bodies, shmodies I hear them say, who? Spirits of the passed of course. I've just returned to Ireland for the Christmas or Xmass, if you like, just to visit family. I find its hard to write when your life's moving forwards at a phenomenal rate. Why is that? Because of interfering spirits. Living in a world where your interventions are welcome is the role of angels or ancestors. The constant reminders from customers that jealousy and rivalry is a common pestilence in their lives, its a constant revelation bringer. Revelations, this is the time. Get out of uncomfortable work, find a job where solitude brings peace, and you'll never have to suffer evermore. Nevermore, will evil bring its footsoldiers into your headspace, physically, sucking your life-force through a straw. Boom! It's the life worth living.

Life's worth living, after you realize you're being conned out of your own self worth! Its inevitable that when you're in your forties, you'll wake up! Realize its all good, and good is where its at. Always has been, always will be. Apocalypse, Ashmocalypse I say. We've been living in modern Human bodies for about 200,000 years or more. Its weird but if you travel back in time far enough, you'll find yourself without a protruding forehead, and quite possibly, one spouse and a large community of equals and opposites. As I write I can feel the intrusion of a thousand years of Karma in the place of some envious Swine, congratulations, another meaning of life, other peoples jealousy. Happy new year! Its 2012 tonight at midnight. Those of us fighting for life's treats and goodies will know what's coming is wholesome and beautiful all in its entirety. The battle rages on, but it will be a battle for fitness and health, power and earthly riches. We all need our gold, our food our clothes, what else do people developed from Caves do? Shop, eat, why even communists shop, believe it or not! Spend energy working to earn energy wearing, eating, and relaxing in the warmth of heat that burns energy, sleeping in beds that give comfort and support. The whole place is supporting us and it's ours to keep. Next life maybe we will have more energy to succeed in energy. Giving, fighting for equality in an unbalanced society, fighting for democracy, for education, for peace, for war, for God knows what. Each lifetime were all coming back, one as a Suffragette, one as a male chauvinist Pig. Who else would fight stronger for equality but the men who have already tasted it and know it will be served. Who else would despise men in this life, that was a Man in the last one, that despised

Women. Some butch Bitch that wants to sleep with your daughters because your ancestors abused hers in a past life. Too heavy a subject? So you're ok with the next generation of party mad Idiots spreading S.T.D.s around, recruiting sensitive people into sexual dysfunction and meaningless organizations flying their meaningless Flags and walking their meaningless Parades. That grimacing Punk with the Pink hair screaming for death and revenge, that's who. Is it you? Are you screaming for revenge on the world, on wholesomeness? On love? On goodness, on equality, or just selling this message to the masses? Are you a Fascist seeking death for all Middleclass? Oh Sisters where art thou?

Anarchists love booze, drugs and self destruction, lost teenagers in an Adult world, bound for skid row and begging for a Dime. So what, big deal, it's all or nothing anyway. Give up the Ghost and get on with making money, that's what it's all about. Recover and take up yoga, never stop banging your drum. Stages.

The initial Punk-Rock movement was based upon not caring about systems and fighting against restrictive middleclass so-called regimes. Let's face it, it didn't make sense pulling the Mickey out of the couch potatoes working classes that were already brainwashed into believing in the power of sloth and booze. The middle class needed to be tested and the powers that be, let punks go to work. "Oi oi!"

Malcolm McLaren was given a shop to do with what he willed for free by an American. He turned it into a shop that sold torn clothes thinking know one would buy them and society would be his art gallery by reacting in shock and horror. People became the art, or were supposed to, until he started selling his stock. So he began to feel like a chosen catalyst for change. He invented by total chance the safety pin t-shirts and torn jeans we see all over today.

People rushed to his shop for clothes that represented teenage angst and rebellious trends representing recreational use of drugs, sex and booze that spanned all classes. Rich and poor both dressed in a uniform of waste and abandon it was Rome all over again, the 7 deadly sins and only on the weekend, everything in moderation especially anarchy. The shop didn't even have a floor, just a huge hole in the ground.

Read into it all you like. Could it represent the void of modernity, parents just getting through the mundane tasks of family life without emphasizing the need for challenge and creativity. Here we are on the brink of change, a new millennium of changes and it's the 80s mentally, not much going on, at all. Extreme measures are needed by us when extreme energies are afflicting us. Until you reject the friends that are unnecessary you will be restricted by their restrictions. Until you restrict the friends you let into your life you'll never really live. When you're young, your lifelong friends help mould you into a confidant person by letting you mould yourself. Letting you listen to your ancestors voices and messages subconsciously, effortlessly and with love and light.

As a lifelong sensitive, I can recall almost any moment from my childhood that my spirit connects to, special places made powerful by ours and other people's experiences. Many memories we recall, of important places will have barriers, hedges, walls, fences e.t.c. to remind our subconscious that the world of our past, although real, is in another time, another place. A safe place, a place of friends and family, if remembering positive things, as we should, as often as possible. Going to Paris to see the Eiffel Tower via visual memory, will impress you with anticipation or disgust. Anticipation of what emotions you will have and/or disgust because it's an iron monstrosity that represents the male dominance that can affect our lives, how can a building or monument that's all old and rusty excite us? It's started hundreds and thousands of marriages! Perhaps you're thinking of unhappy marriages? Are you? Or unhappy people with ugly expressions on their ugly unhappy bitter fake faces? Forget them, forget them and forgive them, they will be happy too.

Write your pretty little faces off and get with the programme. Here's the Man with the plan, the answer for everything. Negative and positive forces are battling around us, metaphysical black dragon verses white dragon. Purity verses putridness. Moderation verses squander and excess. As I write I see a dark shadow above me threatening to kill all around me that I care for.

What's all the fuss? Pestilence is repetition of failure and negative thought-action. Why negativity? Why divils? Why scornful atrocities on a small scale in my personal life? Why the constant threat of lawsuits? Why religious fundamentalism, why man-haters woman-haters, why poverty, why riches? Why blame for African slavery? Sibling rivalry, bigotry, the list is endless; it's exciting really to see it all out there spreading its wings for us all to see. It's on Facebook and when it's lonely or bored, it's infected, it's damned, born of the negative force, the source of negative energies, swirling anti-clockwise for all eternity it is, it's actually damned to repeat its mistakes. No pun, no joke, some energies are actually primed, not temporarily but always and forever. Like a bad puppy that won't ever change, forever, eternal, like life, afterlife, birth-rebirth.

So, why not give temperance a chance. Forget your grammar and listen, for a change. Moderate thought itself. Healers know thought, all about it, where it originates, where it goes back to, what controls thoughts, i.e. energies and spirits. We are all listening to our thoughts all the time. We adhere to their place outside of our heads, outside of our bodies. Swirling around in all directions, living spirit vibrations trying to connect to our bodies and give us itchy scalps! Listen, listen, listen, there was one, here there's one afloat about the floor, close to your spirit animal, or goose, or shoe, or moose or spirit guide. Who knows what we will see when we've been got by one form of thought or another, right?

Something good, ahem for example, A white Dog? A white Dragon? Our true self? Our inner child is and always will be our true self, listening to the spirits of our thoughts. Like Magic, all peril and prejudice one minute, white and light the next. The more sensitive you are the more you're surrounded by thought. Because why, because I wonder, because when?. Because that's life!

Other abused children forget themselves and listen to the left, the past, the ancestral sin, and mistakes our blood relatives made to create us in the first place. Good left-hand thoughts mean we have to let go and open up more to sensitivity and most people think sensitivity is inviting pain, it is. Only because closed minded people are awoken by sensitivity, it reminds them of their first taste of attention which they thought was acceptance as a loud noise in a louder world.

Forget them and move on, most of the time. Have you ever wondered why some people stick in your mind, it's because their stuck in life! Unstick them from your mind and tell them to leave. Turn your Head to the right and immediately your body detoxes all negative psychic energy, I share this secret with many of my customers. Some of them report immediate relief, with amazing feelings of positivity within their stomachs and solar plexus, try it for yourself. Sit up straight, turn your head to the right stick your chest out and breath! Turn your head straight and fell the energy in your pineal gland say, take it on, take on the pressure of thought, deal with the energies of the moment head on. Then turn to the right again, instant relief right? Breath or it wont work.

Also, you can think of anyone in this position and they cannot make you angry, you cannot become emotional when you shut down your subconscious brain. Looking to the right as a meditation throughout the day gives you a chance to rest your mind and stop the incessant babbling caused by psychic rubbish and negative energies/thoughts and actions. Ignore the idiots with a blessing, stop walking past their homes and they will un-stick from your psychic pineal gland quick enough. Stay away from cafes where people you don't like work, or people with an alternative sexual choice or negative sexual vibration and you will find God back in your life; everything is about territory for them (Djin, imps, demons). Forget them and move on. Start helping people who need help, victims.

Stop being a victim and start helping victims to move away from their oppressors. Start small, start with sensitive people. Many sensitive people are targeted by the alternative sexual communities that plague their psychic airspace (many of them, victims of abuse themselves), that's all karma. If you really need some sensitivity, get a massage, hang out with old friends, for a while, if they are un-infected by Millennium djin. Alternative reality is a reality, get with it or be gone. As above, so below!

Move up to bigger things, join Amnesty International, do meals on wheels. At first it will feel un-natural, or fake, until afterwards when you're sick of it, you'll see why. You change, you become aware some of the people you're helping scorn you, that's because their bitter at you for defeating their life-long ambitions of being dominant. Or they hate young hopefuls, or middle class people. Some of us don't care, and that's the secret, its stress that drives them, not us. Them and us, it's what were all against, them being our doppelgangers', nemisi, gatecrashers, or unwelcome strangers or enemies from past lives. People who thrive on stress. Beware of stress, it's a killer. Move on from them, let them go, imagine them enjoying this onslaught of ours against negative energy, our positive constructive community healing, trying to be relaxed energy. They're on caffeine and probably hungover, so they need to drive their sweaty, dirty, bodies on like a mule with tired or sore feet and a rage building up inside that they're willing to spread into our lives like a warted virus. Hey, take a shower, have a cup of coffee, see if I care.

Speed freaks, goodbye. Nothing wrong with high energy, nothing at all. If it's natural, if you've warmed up for it for a purpose, like dancing and stretching, not buzzing about the place like a frizzled-burnt out big bag of nuts. You will find that's what it's all about, energy, good food, organics, getting into the mood and having energy afterwards, not flopping onto the bed or the couch after a frizzled caffeine enhanced energy. I love coffee as much as they do, but I also enjoy positive high energy, not frizzled, like your batteries are on the blink and your head is fried with stress. No, no thanks, goodbye.

Revelations. R-E-V-E-L-A-T-I-O-N-S. It's Eureka Time! Revelations, the book, revealed to me that religion hides the truth. Hidden behind religion is the truth. Simple. Knowing the truth means remembering what many lifetimes have revealed including the stuff we saw whilst in transit. Lovingly accessible to us is this experience for those that have had near death experiences and also, during childbirth. Children we all are, and accessible we that were good, are good. Simples, ahem, simple.

Simple cosmos that's crying out, "It's all in the Hips!" It's all in our left hip mostly; go on ask it, if you want to believe me. "Left hip, what's up?" " It's all good if you believe me" it says. Stomach is close to it, tummy, where our first experiences began. Feeding is energy and life! Personal mothered life! Our personal experience should always be motherly, we should all be motherly to the people we meet otherwise we forget. Rapid forgetfulness is the cause of all sorrow. Tomorrow is full of sorrow for us all, big sorrow and little sorrow. Boohoo's and fearful anxieties that lead to nothing. Life is suffering, but not all bad suffering, some slow moving suffering needs only a little comfort, some fast and needs a major life-change type of pain removal. The first leads us to contemplate the causes of comfort, friendliness, caring and its needs I mean. The cause for comfort, human rights-human wrongs.

Love is a human right. Love is natural to children but not so much with adults. For us it's all about mental stimulation, were more complicated, our emotional/mental immune systems are developed differently. For many people, but what kind of people are you. When I was an actor I played many roles, these roles always became paths. Paths towards a shamanic journey into the characters I played. I always thought it was just coincidence but it emerged that I had already begun the shamanic journey before I became an actor. Therefore murderer, pimp, philosopher, magician, started manifesting for me, actually. At first it was through other people, telling me they were asked to become prostitutes by a pimp. Then by becoming a psychic I learned all about evil/sick/lost people, and dodgy psychics living demonic lives, who were working against good healers/psychics purposefully, but without true awareness that their personalities were truly destructive and possessed by negative habits and entities. Big games for little people.

Psychic detectives are always being harassed by murderous psychics lost in divil-land, sick twisted individuals obsessed with deceit and hell-bent on domination. Microcosmically wow! Mostly just because of their negative conscience waffling on about how weak the good are, how great a bunch of hypocrite's sensitive normally functioning people are.

The battle was within and always will be. The thoughts we have when we look at others are coming from a source, a source of spiritual energy that feeds thoughts. Most people react to your presence with ignorance and therefore cannot allow you time to prepare a positive vibe towards them, it takes practice. Who is watching us/ listening to us? Stopping our thoughts? The little local people, the rats, the dirty rotten apples with hearts that shrink a little every day, god bless em! They have mother-father complexes e.t.c. Who is listening to them? The fat cats, locally, the rotten, money-minded leaders of our locality. The dark side, but not evil. The voices within the double circles of local awareness. The people your mothers are always watching or wary of, or hope your avoiding, people who cause problems for others, just never for themselves, initially.

Alternates to evil, lost souls obsessed with sinful and wicked thoughts or fears always thinking about your sexlife, or who did you sleep with last night? They are always alone even when they're not. They think about your supposed sin. Why? Because if you sleep with someone outside of Marriage you must pay for the sin. They use the bible too, on the rest of us. If you care enough about karma, you may begin to judge people who harass you and see them for what they are, that's judgment that causes you to become alikened to fundamentalism.

You become the one thing you hate the most, a bigot, so beware. What's with the fool who wants you to judge them? They slept with the Djin of Babylon, whom they thought were their wives, the lowlifes of our locality. Waiting for our light to draw near and pounce on our innocence like the plague of the apocalypse, what? You thought they were going to be punished, of course they will be, what's it to you? But not until they have caused punishment first i.e. Our punishment. Confused? For

Women, visa versa.

This is the Apocalypse; this is the Judgment day we have all been brainwashed into hearing. It's not easy though avoiding all Evil as the good Book says we must do in the End of days. But if you do, you will be rewarded with freedom. Trials come from local Neanderthals, local victims of self inflicted abuse, literally, no offence I'm a bit of an ex-self inflicted Moron myself.

Ha! Ha! Say the fathers and mothers of Suburbia. They don't want to hear about Apocalypse in their own bedrooms, they want the dream, ignorance. Ignorance is bliss! My kids are allright, and they probably will be because they were born into middleclass homes, they give to impoverished people and work for charity, because that's what good people do. We help. We are also expected to fight back when offended or insulted but with prayer of magic or through the courts, and just not for any old reason. The courts are not for expressions of anger, psychotherapists are for that. The good innocent victims of underprivileged people are not punchbags to be abused, but try telling that to the schoolyard bullies, they're not listening. They want only what they think they cannot have, freedom! Middleclass? Oh you snobby prig, you snobby mucker, you're an ignorant pig, e.t.c. The world outside must have its say. To itself mostly.

Freedom you say, freedom, but how can I be free? Where can I go? What can I do? Live in Tibet, no they've lost their freedom, I wonder why... live in America the land of the Free? No, that's just a metaphor. Move Planets? Hmm, maybe, but not quite yet, at least not on the earthly plain.

Then what? What's the alternative to living an unhappy life? Could it be the illusive metaphor? Life is suffering. That's what the Buddha said. Life is not about freedom, it's about compromise. When you hit 42 years of age if you're still alive and the booze, drugs, self destruction or abuse or whatever you've been doing up until now hasn't ended your life, then you're still in with a chance at compromise! Yaaaay! I hear you say. Brilliant, now all I have to do is gather up the last remnants of self worth I'm allowed to have from my peers and enemies and move along there's a good boy.

Yes! Eureka! See you again in 1,000 years. You've found the answer to everything and its positive thinking! Intelligence brought on by 42 years from the Bastard brother of wisdom i.e. experience. All idiots can be brought to ground by kindness; they are calling out for it. Most skinhead bully boys never hear or see a kind word from anyone but their wrinkly tattooed hag bigoted troglodytic mothers, if their lucky. Oh it's a work of hate this comediumship! Please forgive me if you're insulted, it's only comedy, I'm a comedium, come on you like a good laugh don't you, while you're sucking on your battered sausages and chips, iinit? Oi! Oi! My ol mans a dustman, he wears a dustman's cap, wahay!

So start trying to find a way to seek their softer side. Just today I noticed a group of idiotic young idiots laughing and staring and turning their heads. Ok, here's a problem I thought, as I ordered my coffee from a nervous offensive insulting looking moronic manager of the local plugs café club of Moronia. Here's a room full of fairly dumb looking people, so I started to work on them, covering my face, or blocking them out with my magazine, but it wasn't until I noticed the waitress (collective consciousness of the damned) was supporting their behavior that I hatched my plan. I thought hey guys, that waitress is female, she doesn't really think your human, she doesn't really care if your girlfriends are her enemies or are in direct competition with her as the future generation of single mothers possessed by boar spirits, she's just trying to recruit you into trouble by causing trouble, by flirting with you and making you look at her large lower-back tattoo saying "aim here", with a hairy growth becoming of a lumberjacks chest, whilst wearing stretch-pants big enough for Pavarotti and giggling. She's more afraid of you than we are. A child of the Virgin Mother still, being a woman and needing respect. But what of self respect?

We are you're brothers, we know people don't ever show you respect unless they want something. All of them relaxed as if they could hear me mentally, this is typical activity from the sensitive sides to insensitive people. Something was speaking to them, voices, the same voices we all hear in our heads, not necessarily psychic, just conscience or inherited conscience.

But they heard and immediately showed compassion towards me. Although I always ask God to forgive my bigoted racist or ignorant descriptions/remarks/thoughts, after I let loose people are very forgiving even the nasty morbidly obese ones, God bless them! And forgive my English! As you read on ask God to forgive me, go on try it, it's addictive and it works. I tried to stop saying to "F" word for years but to no avail, until I started to open my arms to God and ask for forgiveness, it worked and now I very rarely use this word.

It's a bit weird at first, asking God in a blessing kind of way to forgive your tirade of abuse on some unsuspecting innocent, fool or not. In fact I ask to be forgiven every time I call anyone anything. I also forgive people more easily for expanding the view they beset on the rest of us that they inhabit great gifts of insult, physically or mentally. It's a spirit that is granted this task upon us, it has a name and in all cultures cause unhappiness and foul language, insult and hurt. Or its just a negative energy manifestation.

The world we all live in is constantly controlling us. Constantly. Positive and negative. Black days, white days, grey days, black and white days with some grey, golden and silver. Some with all three/five mixed together. As a psychoanalyst of a sort, being a professional medium working on a 14 hour day, filled with a lot of snoozing, every day I know that all healers have developed good workable techniques that subdue the anger of their clients. The public at large need subduing because they act like victims. Nazis acted like victims and look what happened to them, they became victimizers, that became victims of almost self inflicted abuse, Nihilists. They screamed for help, with war, anger, atrocities, sensitivity to foreign and domestic supposed abuse even. Much like the lesser Nazis we suffer on a daily basis. They were abused, in their own minds, abused by privileged people. People who had a developed society, a developed sense of worth of self respect, of spirituality. Negative energy found its way into the hearts and minds of every German it could and hey presto! Bullies. Bullies with tribal tattoos, tattoos of a race that would have eaten us if we ever crossed paths.

Bullies that were sure that sensitive spiritual beings must suffer and die. Bullies with a vendetta, who tried to take over the world. Bullies try to take over our lives too, now more than ever. It's all ok, it's all allright, don't panic, the crazy mans just babbling on about his usual obsessions, his imaginary friends and his obvious tendency to moan on and on and on incessantly about his own problems obviously. Ve can sit on him and fart in his general direction later, after we have had our burger and chips, smoked a fag and bought the daily Star, coz were special, burrrrrp!

Oh yea! Yes, yes, it's true, the truth is spoken, indeed it is. Spoken, in the beginning was the word, but what of its origin? Original thoughts don't exist. They are found by spirits created by energy, the big bang, gravity, gasses, metals, waters, winds, pressure, God is pressure, intuition is Gas, psychic ability is hormonal reaction and vibration, divine divination is mature logic and reasoning, attention to detail and conscience. Our greatest fear isn't not surviving evil; it's being allowed to survive it. Being left behind after all the young heroes and heroines are long dead. Left in apathy to veg out on the couch singing praises of modernity's hex/ageism. Some 85 year old soldiers are still well able bodied, having fought the physical manifestation of evil, because their modern colonial ancestors used to be that manifestation of evil. Now they're so easily forgotten by society, especially societies rejects. More to the point humanities rejects, idiots and failures selling their philosophies through their backsides. Brainwashing is and always has been a huge part of our daily existence, it lives and breathes in the bodies of lost souls and imbeciles (Not the technical term) Politicians(Pun)

If you're good, now in this millennium time, good things...eventually, will happen. It's just around the next corner, I promise, but first there's a large amount of corners ahead and I'm afraid, no end to many of them. It's metaphorically eternal. One way or the other, at least from my experience of life has shown me so. One way or the other, no compromise. Compromise and be damned supposedly, if you continue down the wrong route. Forces at work will serve to prove, to no end, that the end is in sight. It, the forces at hand, positive or negative will serve to prove one way or the other to lead the way. So much so in metaphors that will manifest in the physical plane, mostly on Sundays. The day of rest.

So great! I've settled into this island of crazy Arabs and am being constantly stalked by the spirits of apocalypse, but in a quite extraordinary way. Just behind my house is a road and the traffic noise cannot be heard, so it feels like alien spacecraft taking off from my next door neighbors house when they turn the corner. Giving alien energies the wondrous opportunity to listen to my every thought, but only when there's a car or truck around, interesting. Alternate Universes? Most probably. Sacrifice, is today's request, sacrifice of all unnecessary relationships including unnecessary contact with unwelcome people.

Millennium-end of days. Feeling good about it when you're up, down about it when you're down. Writing this isn't easy with all the opposing forces around. It feels like lost children looking for immediate justice. Justice for what? Being self destructive, even writing has become laborious, but I'm still high from the positive energies available, like opiates to sedate us from the cancerous other half's out there. Ireland is absolutely high and low, opposing forces at war with each other for your eternal soul. Spirits of the elements really, full to the brim with earth energy and filled with the joy of life, wanting for nothing but the spirit world and high energy. Full of anxiety like you've never seen! High and low, high and low, like the sea.

Land of elementals. Spirits of air, Earth, water, fire, all the circle of life. Malta is more relaxed and able to give you the choice, for a plateau of energy rather than the full on air energy of Ireland. Plus in countries that allow for space, you are at the mercy of that element of air spirits. There is a different reaction depending on who's out there in the element of air. How they allow for their bodies to be used for positive or negative forces. How we react or act upon their effects on us. How we use the same elemental spirits to act upon them, with love and light, Eureka! Its is simple, and it is work. That's why its hard to function these days, because all that we do, all that we are is light and love. Every thought, every action, every deed of darkness and hate. Alternatively of course.

Here and now I'm writing away for love and light as a professional tarot reader, member of spiritualist unions and a practicing light-magician with the Esoteric order of the Golden Dawn. No longer can the inner critic play the same role in the mindset of this new world of ours (Our organization) angels, angels, angels, that's what its all about. No bad stuff, that's just hype.

What everything is about, what we are based upon, the representation of enlightened beings struggling to make sense of a world on the edge. This planet is still going places, and no, were not going with it, not forever, that's for the next generation. Next life for you, not this one. This ones gone a little pear shaped. Lets concentrate on the next one. After all that's what we did in the last life, wait for the paradise plane to free us of this inconstant spiral of repeated mistakes, spiritual and physical DNA faults, trial and error, pain and loss, love, tears and life! Family.

We watch movies, we watch plays, read books, converse, complain, look for concealment. Experiment, watch others play or exploit the earth's recourses. People are open now mentally, listen to their inner reasoning, ask if they support life and Earth watching, yet still use gas or coal or oil to heat their homes. There's always a little hypocrisy in our lives. Conspiracy aside, we are allowed to enjoy life even if that means triviality, conversation with waiters and waitresses that could grow platonically become important relationships.

Not like the movie "As good as it gets" That's actually about wrong decisions, how many people do you know that end up this way? The true meaning behind our outside lives is enjoyment. Were always waiting for that next coffee or chocolate bar or sugary treat or natural high or herbal tea. Creatures of a sort we are waiting to be taken away from this life, away from the other living beings, off into another world we secretly know to exist. I've just spent the last two years studying constantly for an organization that deals with psychic development and magic in the hope that I can enjoy the freedom power gives us. I did have an education indeed from magical sources(very little difference to aura seeing and meditation) and luckily don't have to worry so much as to the in-depth need to study constantly anymore, by choice. I still want to write and have decided that half way is usually where a medium likes to be, so half way is where I'll stay.

Working away on what we are meant to work away on is necessary for ourselves, not for our peers. Life throws us a bone once and a while and we need to see that, lay back and enjoy it for all its worth. I spent years working constantly to escape the powers controlling my life and couldn't.

CHAPTER FOUR

Psychic Blocks.

Psychic blocks are a new revelation to me. I have found out that these are a normal part of a psychics path. I never heard of them until I started to study magic. Now as I write this I can see that this revelation itself is affected by what I would call blind spots. I think psychic blocks are impish and partly connected to the blind spot in our eyes for one part. This energy is constantly getting in our way, slowing things down and allowing slow spirits to serve as servants for the mission of psychic blocking. The masters of the world order are served in one part because they are still jealous of the freedom people have that have made them rich. The source of blocking energy is anti-life force (or possibly necessary), this energy is sufficient to slow down the human race enough to repel over population and is therefore serving a just cause. Plus it gives us pace to the week whenever things slow down or pace naturally, there's always an energy around. A deed, a word, an action, a reaction, from humans and from the elements around us.

Many of my readings start with the clients saying "No" to absolutely everything I say. At first, you think their being obtuse, or stubborn, or ignorant, they may well be if you get stuck, but the trick is, just keep going. For example, "Hello, your Mothers name is Mary" the client says "No", its Mary Ellen, well we call her Mary, but that's not her name. OK, "Is there a Pat in the family"?, the client says "No" and subsequently says no to everything else I say. Until after about 10 minuets', I go back over the names, as I had clearly known they were experiencing a psychic block, and I have a little fun with them and a say uncle Pat says that your second auntie Joan says that Peter, your ex boy-friends dog Jasper says hello" And they say "Oh my God, yes Uncle Pat" Have you Googled me?" Sure like I have the time to do that.

Have you been connecting to your fellow beings as an equal? Giving your time to something now that you're ready to? As a reiki healer, or psychic medium, as a healer of light and life forces of nurture and discipline. Blocked energies are all attributed to our place in the world. When we find ourselves, our life plan, when it finds us. Our community can help remove blockages by supporting our cause, our percentage of effort to help other professional beings. Keeping the mob mentality of clients at bay. The surge of chaotic manipulation in itself can create a new wonder in us about what inspired humans to become aware of the need to understand the effects of moving in straight lines. Why did the Romans build straight roads, industriousness, awareness of secretive informative structures that annihilate small mindedness. The whole bartering with the minute step by step, penny by penny, number by number, person by person, one step at a time collectively, together under one rule, voted in by one vote at a time. A senate set up by the Druids, who were far superior to any world religion I might add.

Becoming a healer brings isolation, perhaps only in your workspace. With isolation comes revelations and temptations. The awakening of the mooladhara chakra during the day is part and parcel of you daily energizing work, with that part of the body we have indigenous confrontations with sexual energy for example, if its under control, great! Lets work on your strengths, if you have any that is, as you get older your body needs more purity, otherwise its becomes over sensitive and your pocket suffers, your mind suffers, your clients suffer, your reputation suffers, the list is endless, but flexible. This is where it's helpful to have experience with city workers, disaster management, binmen, electricians, policemen, traffic wardens, road workers; they all represent the Zen of a healthy working system, i.e. White corpuscles. Collective consciousness manifesting as a unified web of spiders. Rise with the golden dawn.

There are worlds within worlds standing in our way, even in our own lives. The world of the heart, the inner child, controlled by ancestors voices, wanting only what's best for the family, not necessarily us, the individual (Oxymoron) Our own ancestors may favor someone else in our family network over us and help them by acting as a spirit guide, but not with our success in mind. Who cares why, I've just told you, its not in our favor.

Politics starts in the home, in our heads, in our bodies, in our spiritual existence. Why? Because you're probably not the head of the family, you're probably the middle child, the black sheep, the outcast, the source of all blame, why? Because only elders can give you a reason to learn the hard way, nobody else will. Your grandparents have psychic rites over your mind, they are given this by natural selection. Its genetic and scientific, even the greatest minds are still controlled by their parents thoughts or their grandparents thoughts and act or react to them accordingly, it a good thing. If you're a child you're expected to do what you're told, nobody likes individuality, its not good for the family. Society is affected by this because we all have families. You may find that Orphans are supremely individualistic and severely independent, they have to be.

If your controlled and you know it, make elders your bread and butter, become a psychic medium, beat them at their own game. Your grandparents are only defending their own children, your uncles and aunts, so don't think for one minuet that they will help their grand children more than their own offspring. Think and think and contemplate the reality that makes complex emotions into complex survival mechanisms. If you want to be wealthy you have to understand the politics of wealth, the power of wealth, the freedom it brings and the entrapment it brings.

Money is the route to Philistines that are only interested in money, not art. Pop music sells, sex sells, slavery sells, booze sells, drugs sell, herbal remedies sell, yoga sells, meditation sells, everything sells. Buddhist monasteries sell, religion sells, spiritualism sells, babies sell, fashion, war, sugar, land, countries, roads, borders, seas, oceans, telephone wire, satalights, poetry and books, everything.

Freedom sells, chaos and anarchy sell too. Cavemen were buying their futures before they took their first step. Life is ruled by thousands of hidden worlds, all of them are based on a use once then replenish basis. Air is spent in our lungs and we repay it with recycled gases, we serve to replenish the earth itself with our bodies to nourish the earth itself, and were bio-degradable, were organic!.

Thousands of explanations as to the origin of products and produce, manmade or natural. Made for a purpose, not just for enjoyment, but for cultivation. Storing for a rainy day. For our future generations well being, welfare. Aha! A plan! Cave men, were not just living in the moment, but were planning their futures all along. Plotting their futures, for their offspring, thinking of tomorrow. Killing for tomorrow.

Their enemies, dying for a great tomorrow. Therefore war is good. Killing is necessary to make room for more offspring and more power…its political, its politics at its most basic level is survival. Not many people kill themselves because they want to make room for the overpopulation of our Planet, do they? You would think some tree huggers would be so gracious! Revolution from evolution. Want to live for the moment? Be a free spirit? Flee from responsibility? Love everyone? Somebody somewhere is going to test your metal. That's for sure.

In fact, that's another of the many meanings of life. As we meander down the road through 20.. into 20.. were entering the forbidden zone. The void, the solitary collective place of our ancestors. (20.. means whatever year your reading this.)

All things known to man are revealed constantly through communication. Ramifications and timing, you will find are part and parcel of the seller's market. The questions that pass through the mind of the inexperienced naïve beings that wander through life looking to get lucky by suckling on the misfortune of others.

The questions we hopefully have ourselves found floating precariously close to our IDs, our conscience, our inner mind and rejected. As you grow older and more mature. Opportunity is an organic synthesized thing that only the truly adept sorcerer can make the most of. Opportunity to refuse the first offerings in the hope of a more tepid choice. You will see after many years of survival that indeed, something's come to he who waits. It's a beautiful world we live in after all. Yet when all is said and done it's only an unusual place some of the time, it's always a mystical realm of possibility all of the time. People do suffer consequence but also, people do show their place in our lives via curiosity. They love to know if we are in the wrong place at the wrong time and are lemmings for disaster, especially other peoples foibles.

The true meaning of life is there are thousands of meanings to life. Otherwise we would be bored with just survival. Even animals play, explore, and plan their live through instinct. We are made as humans in animal bodies and are gifted with instinct and intuition. The constant changes in the astral area around our heads means that we can't pin down any thought process. Were organic and so thought makes our lives more dangerous if our world can suddenly change from one instant to the next because of outside influences like other people. Curiosity can overcome some peoples thought processes and get them all a fluster when free thinking individuals like ourselves veer too close, its dangerous. That's the meaning of life (Like many others) millennium life, its all about survival. Surviving other people. Other people's curiosity isn't through programming by the divine computer; it's inherited by suffering and experience, the bastard brother of knowledge. The illegitimate metaphorical sibling of all philanthropic people, disgruntled vagrants on the path to selfish deterioration, when all around them are family trying to help steer them back on the path to good health.

Experienced curiosities are the cause of many creative ideas, like selling sex, drugs, water and air

(2nd World War-Germany) It's a buyer's market meaning you the consumer, you'll be respected by the rich if you make them rich. The greatest conspiracy is the invisible one. For example "Aliens" aliens are us. We come back thousands of years from now in not only UFOs, but light airplanes, helicopters and jets. Why? How? Time machines. We've already been back to Italy and The French Riviera about 600 years ago to plan the expensive holiday resorts built there. The hotels and yacht ports around the world are all making big money for the people who plan them and own them. Casinos make millions per year, who else can afford time travel other than millionaires. The big man at the top has ancestors in the future that are all connected to him via Freemasonry e.t.c. By the time we work it out we will be gone, our future generations will be here to scratch their heads and figure it all out. 1000s of years from now we will have colonized all the dead planets out there and built cities with millions of people who believe in the stories of "Earthlings" out there in the great unknown.

Life is what it is, there are other dimensions of course, 1000s of them. All of them are manifestations of mutation. "Mutants!" Mutations occur when our spirits are unclean or unhealthy and therefore we manifest in the spirit world as unlike our true selves. As the spirit world is now molecularly conjoined with the physical plane, especially pre-2012 these manifestations are becoming more and more relevant as we progress or digress according to our physical activities morally.

Revelations make it easier. As 2012 progresses into the future were all alike in many ways. Some of us are accepting a new existence whilst our old existence is playing out. Were connecting to others easier that usual. Creating the illusion of closeness, or creating the feeling of closeness, as much as we would like to, whatever's comfortable for each person. Constructively of course. Beware the pain of loss, the fear of letting go, the need for hormones and endorphins outside of exercise, it leads to failure. We are now expected to achieve great heights after Millennia of human failure, trial and error, common good, give us a chance. We have had all the chances we could possibly have, now is the time for flight or failure, perhaps it has always been so. Do or die forevermore, not so easy being a New World Order super successful drone is it?

Intense feelings are commonplace for some of us in the healing industry. Were aware of some amazing truths, truths that we are constantly working with day in, day out. Most of the time there is always a need for sensitive awareness of our surroundings. Depending on where you live, who surrounds you and how well they communicate with each other. For the moment the rat race is on like never before, there's always a need for speed, whatever role you're playing. Constant motion in a world where the wicked never rest, until they splurge out on the weekend and spend another Sunday sleeping in. Missing the world outdoors and desperately trying to defeat the rest of us with tiredness and lobotomizingly boring hangovers. The hangover of a lifetime is now upon the whole Human Race, after only 100 years or so of pollution and War, we have a Mega clean up on our hands, a possible manifestation of negative molecular energy floods beyond scientific recovery that's set to hit over the next 50 years or so, the list goes on. So we haven't got time to wait for tired people to catch up, we all get tired sometimes, but when recovered are back to work and busy. Harmonious changes all begin with War of some sort. They are connected to nature- everything is.

Fire Ahead!

Saving ourselves for better times, its over in a heartbeat and takes a long time. With this in mind our futures are poised for some changes and some trials. Before the Apocalyptic millennium I found my friends were few, but those that were, where true. The meaning of life is friendliness in our day, our community, our macro and microcosms. Our attitudes to others gives us some taste of success and virtue. In reversal, we are subjected to the twisted version that others choose to use against us, why? Politics. The small world of personal politics I have mentioned in my other books " "A Mediums Dream" and "Hawk" But here, I will mention again the path I find myself on is steadily progressing on to bigger and better things, thank God.

Moving from one country to another for example, studying different cultures and how they enable people to grow or decline in fashion. At the moment I'm living in Biarritz in the Basque Country, France. Mind blowingly beautiful views that stagger the imagination, history to die for and city planning second to none. The attitude to life here is very, very different to what I am accustomed to, no talk of suicide along with the weather etc. (although, after 3 weeks here, I've noticed, they keep it all bottled up inside) there's definitely a collective consciousness that supports positive thinking, imagine that! Bizarre.

I have seen people's reactions to negative thoughts and most people are completely aware of allowing positive thought mechanisms to over-ride the negative. A Choice to ignore negative energy because of an awareness of conscience, brought on by a society that is successful. A successful society builds well-being and a good philosophy for life. Well to do, comfortable, educated and reasonably happy general population, depending on where you live. A generous point of view? Absolutely. A positive do what thou wilt… be good and good things will happen…keep it simple and allow yourself to be carried along by serendipity, it does work, there is hope, why didn't I move here 20 years ago, I would have had a life! Why? (Of course I'm just on a high because I'm in a new place, reality will set in soon, I'm sure) Karma, life lessons and the bastard brother of wisdom, experience. My own culture had things it wanted me to learn. historically it takes 300 years of freedom to recover from 100 years of oppression, so Irelands 26 counties have about 1100 years to go before we recover completely. About the amount of time percentage wise G.B had to recover from Roman occupation, or "Alien" occupation. Language changes created by Latin affected most of Europe.

Ireland will never be the same all over, but will represent slow recovery all the same. Where there is blood there is war. Here in the French governed side of The Basque Country it's still quite traditional, without any reactionary factions as far as I can see or hear. Not like in the Spanish Basque country which to my mind resembles Northern Ireland, where I was born. As a spiritualist psychic with great interest in the eternal soul, I do communicate with the spirits of my forefathers from time to time and have had clear messages about The Basque Country in Spain from alternate sources. Powerful spirits visiting me at night just outside my window, one huge man who manifested as the spirit of a pig that represented his hatred for the Basques. I think he was a Spanish cop that was murdered by ETA, the Basque separatist group. Scary visitation indeed, but fascinating all the same. A man that needed to express his fascistic pride and self-respect, a cry for the domination of people who want independence and cultural freedom that I can understand. I know how the evil one ply's his trade and what anger can do to a country, especially a country that had left others well enough alone for many, many, years.

Take Tibet for example, why are they occupied? Karma. They invaded China eons ago, so have to repay the bad done there. The Vikings that marauded Ireland came to call it their own and defended us from Viking Hoards! In the name of Christianity with Brian Boru a Viking King. The circle comes round, but so few of us are open minded enough to see it, inevitably leading to opposition, and that's another form of personal politics. More than an interest have we all, some of the time, not all of the time. When Oliver Cromwell entered Galway City walls, he was really just freeing Ireland from the Gaelic-Anglo-Normans that built towns and had castles pitted here and there in pure Gaelic country really. He was in many ways the beginning of Irish freedom, ironic, isn't it? Round 1691, about 300 years ago. Crom the God of Paganism returns to oust the Catholic foreign God and smash his temples and deface his icons and statues just like the Christians did to Croms icons and temples.

Its blatantly obvious to me that names mean something more than their worth. In fact, the origin of names is a spiritual meaning pertaining to the personality and power of the person and our role in life. A doctrine we can all attain, is the meaning of our given name.

Depending on for whom the bell tolls, political drama may be the only kind of politics some people endure, or create. Having spent many years being surrounded by young people on the wrong path in life, manly flat-mates I wouldn't necessarily have chosen, given the choice. Just like family. So, called friends that again were only necessary for a limited time because they were fellow musicians. As any artist will know, artists are the lowest form of life (metaphor) drugs, drink, hashish-long term users. Actors that would overstep a dead body if it would get them an audition. We have all done stupid things and the reasons are now clear to me. Voices in our heads, telling us what to do, voices that get us to do things because otherwise we would have to think for ourselves. Weird. Weirdness rules our lives for much of our adolescent years, even into our adulthood, even when we have left our old lives far behind, the voices of unreasonablity are echoes in the darkness, skeletons in the closet. Deep messengers that return when they feel like it, on a whim or when were under duress with stress, or loneliness, or hormonal awakenings that create habits of repetitive compulsion. The world of a saint can be very ominous and dangerous. Having to live in a world of perfection compromised by the weaknesses of misguided indiciplined opposites, especially within your own bodies. Self-realized puritanical beings with all the trappings of a universal psychic power way beyond the saints of our past. Reiki healing, remote viewing, clairvoyance-audience-sentients, spirit mediums, yoga and martial art. We are all becoming the saints of the past without realizing the powers involved are enormous and demand a discipline that is sadly lacking in all of us.

Opposites react, where confrontation exposes us to each other. Were all on the road now my friends, the more you travel, the less time you have to waste, or for wasting, the older you get, the wiser you should be, unless you're a fool. Fool is wise in the moment, but not until the next fool life lesson, or constant learning experience leads to fool suffering. In itself foolishness is in us all. When we look into the world of others we see them for who they are especially at that moment in time. As we grow wiser we start to analyze people when we meet them, are they exactly what I'm looking for? Are they? If not shouldn't I be civil and move on? I should, I will, I have done and I am. What next? Love, that's what next, honesty and fearlessness. Perhaps the person I just met could have been somebody special, (But resembles a dog or a rabbit more than a human) something special, but what are we looking for, what I'm looking for is very different from what most people are looking for. Almost ready for the next spiritual level? We wonder. Rhetorical quests in the metaphysical molecular reality.

Lourdes

I've just returned from Lourdes, went for a moonlight swim and wrote that last paragraph. I've been told by certain publishers that I'm too Joycean and dense and I should have more chapters in my books and more headings for each subject. "Too many words", one secretary told me, then she lost the pages she typed for me and her boss threatened to call the police if I didn't leave their office, imagine that! Anyhow, Lourdes was fantastic, getting there was a nightmare. The battle axe at the ticket counter, (Obliviously in league with the imp master of ignorance and anxiety) made me repeat the word Lourdes 10 times, until she said oh Lourdes! in a very aggressive and loud manner in as thick a French accent as she could, to emphasize the fact that she was telling me, in her own way, that I was pronouncing it wrong. (The Devil) No train to the first stop at Bayonne, had to catch a bus at 11:00 am, driven by Freddy Krueger on acid in the Monaco Rally, stopping at around 20 stops, even though there were no people waiting at the stops and I was the only passenger on the bus. I was Sea sick after 10 minutes and wanted to get off and go home, the suspension was that of a carnival ride and every turn, which were many and constant made my stomach rise up to my throat. I knew the Beast was working hard to stop me getting to the Virgins Sanctuary, especially when we had only driven 1 mile distance towards my destination, but had driven 6 miles through the maze of suburban estates along his route, got to the train station with 5 minutes to spare (that insane bus journey took 1 hour).

If any of you have gone to Biarritz and taken the bus to Bayonne, you too would agree, I am making no exaggeration, whatsoever. The train journey was magnificent! Passing beside mountain streams and forests, higher and higher through the mountains, wow! Got to Lourdes and was amazed at the views of the mountains. Did the tour and took the bath. The bath is basically where you're supposed to be cured of all that ails you, cancer, spinal problems, paraplegia, among others.

Well I did feel the power of belief all around, from some people. I was aware of spiritual energy clearing negative spirits away. When it eventually came to my turn it was 3:30 pm, I entered the bath chamber, took off my clothes, they give you a kind of loin cloth apron to wear, then entered the water where you say a prayer of choice. Mine was Michael the Arc Angel of course, which I know very well but couldn't remember a word of there and then. They almost carry you forward and plunge you into very cold water, wash a little, have a drink, and say "Blessed Mother Mary and Blessed Saint Bernadette. That's it, I do feel better and some of my aches and pains are gone. So, if you want to know is it worth it, go.

Although being used to swimming in cold water and showering in freezing water, I entered the bath with silent ease, whilst all around me where the operatic whoops of ooah! Woo! Woah! From all the other men entering the cold baths beside me. One of the guys helping me even pushed me deeper as if confused as to why I was so silent, what's wrong with this guy he was thinking, his fellow helper even took his hands off me and said, that's enough, its ok, nod, nod, wink, wink, who's that fool more like.

Don't start thinking that you're a Saint now or anything, but faith is the key. That's why much healing is called faith healing. If you don't believe in something, you don't have the right to criticize it or give an opinion, that just insults the intelligence of the people who do. They have experience in spiritual things that many critics do not.

Is having to place headers on each subject's paragraph anally retentive. For those morons out there, it's a metaphor and yet they shouldn't feel like theyre too stupid, it may lead to mental constipation, a kind of a super genius after all. Stupid people are a wonder to us all, as making an art of figuring out how to avoid becoming stupid is what most of my work is about. The constant interference from idiots during the millennium Apocalypse of the 21st century is why were all suffering on a daily basis(Pun) Where I live now has some crazy weird idiotic moronic mentality I have to be honest. It probably stems from opposites. I mean this Planet Earth, right here and now is brimming with both promise and total failure, or at least what I deem total failure. Religious fundamentalism from the left and the right. Fascistic nationalism which is a choice, believe it or not(Joke) For those of you too dumb to understand political humor, what? Dumb? Me?

Anal retentiveness is a recognizable metaphor created by the one and only psychoanalyst himself, revealer of the collective animus, Freud. Those of us educated by coffee table worldly interests already know who I'm talking about and yes, I am patronizing the idiots reading what they see as insufferable hogwash and babble, after all somebody has to take our place in scapegoat Heaven (Oxymoronic self-debilitating dope heads) i.e. living Hell, or as the original version (Viking) Hel a goddess that controlled the gates of her kingdom, her name is Hel, the Goddess. Master of low vibration truths

Maybe Helga is attributed, who knows, who cares, we all do. You'll have to forgive my humor if you are unfathomably dumb, don't worry you probably inherited it from your forefathers. Heh! I'm not talking about you, you're special, your intelligent, you've seen what the world is about, you know all that's real can be touched with the hands, felt in the stomach and like a monkey you know that most things can be broken. God bless you. We understand what stress can do, and what insensitive free-thinking Philistines are trying to do to this, your country. Is there another world out there, do other people really exist? Are they just figments of my imagination? Probably. Maybe were all aliens and the end really is nigh. Ha! Ha! You wrote the Bible; your father is a goat and your Mother understands you. I am God! I am huge, I can! Yes I can! Glug, glug, fart, burp, pee, laugh, fanatic, fascist, moron. Fifty percent of The Earth's population thinks in this way, man woman and child. There we have it, half the population of The Earth is anally retentive, it stands to reason that we must allow them to be and leave them to it. Not judging them, just making a conviction to their ploy on reason, literarily. In their next life, they will learn by overcoming the obstacles their forefathers have laid down for them, otherwise they would be damned to eternal stupidity in a world that understands what they do is wrong irreguardless of their own idiotic understanding, or lack of it, fact.

Fact

Just making headlines to sedate the compulsions of my future Publishers.

You never know this could be the making of a new style for me. Ahh yes the world of professionalism does indeed decree the knowledge of facts (Hence the header) although in the psychic world the figure and facts are defined by the morals of the practitioners. The definition of humanity also falls into categories

Categories that pigeon-hole each and every one of us, eventually; peer pressure predicts some people's morals and places pigeon holes in conjunction with where they think others should go. For example alternative sexual choices voiced via the media are always and forever trying to force their opinions on impressionable teens by not allowing them to make up their own minds. At least in the media, where fashion dictates what the square world thinks "Natural" sexual choices are. This in itself allows some people to find themselves being pushed away from heterosexuality or bisexuality even before they have had the chance to experience it.

Why? Idiot drive (Hey, who needs headings) idiot drive is a control mechanism that many people are affected by, it's a spiritual energy that has to enter the body mostly through the left side of the body, right side of the brain. If you're truly psychic and professional in your approach to all things mental, you will slowly start to see similar patterns forming in other people. If you're lucky (So few psychics are) you won't have to open your metaphorical sphincter to learn it the hard way. We are all surrounded by evil souls bent on total domination of our character. Souls directly connected to our families and their place in the world. As too the families of the damned souls that troll us. Alcohol, always the reason. Alcohol and the spirits that reside within a torn soul, a battered life an a demon bent on revenge, coming your way in the clowns spectacle that is the millennium! Oh look! A politician who promises deliverance! Were saved!

Peer pressure is a fact; don't deny it, anyone that failed in first year psychiatry will tell you. Certain famous celebrities (David Bowie) may have been at the forefront of the sexual revolution, they did represent certain genres of sexuality, at least sexual experimentation i.e. Pan sexuality or bisexuality for many people was and is just a phase of their (Your) lives. Many of these celebrities returned to absolute heterosexuality including their audience after they had their fill and wanted a reasonably normal existence. Irregardless of angry outbursts from other factions, nobody really cared, because these famous people didn't endorse an absolute crossover to any monomaniacal beliefs or fascistic beliefs all too prevalent in the media. There are no ex-bi parades.

Now why would this be? Hmmm, nobody's really interested in reasonable heterosexuals keeping themselves to themselves, are they? No, they're not, and why? Money, sex sells, money, short term solutions to long term problems that destroy their own objectives in the process. Also, any so called hetro that talks about alternative sexual appetites is voicing a subconscious need to experiment themselves. The power of belief is strong, even the belief that something un-natural is good, yes something's are good, temporarily. In a thousand years of temporary existence earthlings have had many times throughout history invented or reinvented themselves, so they think.

That's just it, in fact, people don't do the thinking, something else does, spirits. Spirits give many the understanding, if they choose to ignore or pretend that spirits don't exist, they will not exist. Responsibility de damned, and they are. That's karma. Leave the effects of living a certain way to the wayside and ignore the facts, and be damned the future of unwitting naïve others to their own undeveloped sweet will. Peer pressure relinquished logic and responsibility, the rich become richer etc. But the facts have returned to force the hell of accepting what goes around comes around to those that do not wish to deal with fact. The fall of the Towers of Babel represent man and his ego suffering even though they choose not to. It's again a fact that irresponsible peer choices lead to side effects all the time, small warnings to people that hate warnings and revolt against reason and logic, for sex, money, power, lethargy, beer, nicotine, ignorance, sloth and war etc.

This Earth with all its potential as far as I can see, will always have its failures, so why not give in, have a whale of a time, kill all the whales and be damned, many people have, so why not you eh? Why not save the whales and smoke yourselves to death on hashish and skunk weed watching the discovery channel, it's a cry for help, and that's a fact. Impervious to psycho analysis and the facts. Fact, fact, fact. Enough, justification, put us back in the trees with our thumbs where the sun doesn't shine, and leave us to it, we belong there, so, some of us do. Many of these people have called me a monkey, caveman, or an animal, or worse. Truth is, now I accept the challenge of being tested by bullies, especially because I know how much they long for power. Small people allow more import-ant people to support their bullying, hence regimes of fascism in our microcosms (That's the local personal world we live in) This is becoming my favorite pastime, surviving idiots, their addictions and their abilities to think, because they don't have the capacity for thought any more. The forces around us now since Jacobs Ladder, the beginning of the Y.2.K. spiritual virus, have put a stop to cer-tain peoples thought processes, too radical a belief? Or fact?

You, think about it, it will take a couple of decades and a few books on the subject, believe me. That's what were here for, to think. That's the meaning of life, thought. What we choose to allow into our heads, affects our personalities. We have and always will have voices telling us what thought to take in, if we think about it. We live in a world now that tells us what to think, its even getting us to use the newspapers as we read to give us certain information sporadically. For example, your on the train, you've got a newspaper with you, you open it and the first thing your eye falls on is "He's got Herpes" Or "She's pregnant" or whatever the energies connecting to us are willing to oblige. This is called divination, shamans practice the art for thousands of years and now in this new era, we are all open to it. Everybody. Our mental capacity is primed for new experiences through technology and our understanding of other people through our thought alone. We are being awoken to our own selves constantly and are becoming more sensitive to stress and person-ality clashes in the workplace and perfect strangers outside of it. At times it can be overwhelming for no real reason, but we are collectively supporting each other with positive thoughts too. It's the time of revelations-Jacobs Ladder, planetary alignment, my favorite topic. This Book is a higher level from my last one, as I develop, so too does my art, my readings with tarot and psychic me-diumship. All of us are being prepared for Purgatorial existence, the absolute reckoning of the soul, the time of awakenings, the Hebrew belief is that this is the 1000 years of women. A period on earth where we can all experience our potential. Great! All we can do for now is "Keep going" Change must come with abysmal failures, ignorance, insult and constant effort. Especially with people who think they need help to shine, or that other people need to support them if they are to succeed. Whatever happened to hard work!

Il Paradiso

What a heading, Paradise! Its all in the mind, some say, so it is. Paradise doesn't come cheap, so they say. It's a road built on wisdom, the golden child of reason. The golden child of wisdom, is reason and purpose, you'll see it on a miniature calendar on somebody's office desk someday, (Hope) Hope springs eternal, hope floats, when I was an adult, I remembered to dream. I let go of fear and started to float, a little, I'm floating now, can you feel it? I just came indoors from a short walk outdoors in my bare feet, to check out the stars in the humid heat of an October night in Biarritz.

Goddess, yes, its nice allright. People have lived here for 200,000 years! (Neanderthals, cavemen, then humans 20,000 years ago) Many of our ancestors came from here, they live here still, for them its normal and that helps to keep it real. I'm sure in January it'll be "caold" as we say in Ireland. Still, this heat in winter is Paradise, even walking into the centre during the day in the heat and seeing all the happy faces walking by the beach reminds me of that Robin Williams movie "What dreams may come" There's a scene with people in Paradise floating around and happy faces everywhere. Its just like that here, I've died and gone to Heaven, and the scenery is absolutely magnificent, if I make it I'm going to buy a place here and settle in for the great beyond, ohh yes! Revelations 2012, its apt, its happening now, to you, to us all, hard times, easy times, good and evil, side by side, get into it, were being weighed and measured by Anubis and St Peter, one way or the other.

So which side are you on? If you cant serve two masters, and every weekend you feel the pull, towards the pub, disco or next sexual encounter e.t.c. perhaps you have left this consumer life behind.

Living the life of a disciplined spiritual person, or married with kids? Celibate pseudo Buddhist angelic being surviving in this world as a HSP. (Hyper sensitive person) Always vigilant, watching for spiritual energies and clearing away negative energy naturally. Incense burning as you see in the Far East. It clears the space and keeps negative spirits out. Not like in the west where any mention of "Spirits" and your ostracized from the normal non-believers, even though in their naivety their "Church" adopted incense burning 2000 years ago. We are the new generation of free thinkers living in an anally retentive society that is emotionally dysfunctional and devoid of any real spiritual guidance. As it is, so it is meant to be.

Hey! Its great! I'm criticizing the mob mentality, I'm doing what I've always wanted to do, destroy my enemies moral! Obliterate the bacteria! Kill all opposition! That's what their doing to you and me, we need to fight back. Greenpeace is, fighting against ignorance and greed. But how much good are they actually responsible for? People are allowed to lose their humanity, its legal in some countries, hey, all countries. Some countries even endorse it, communist countries, capitalist countries, socialist countries, republics, dictatorships....Perhaps in the future we will give up our free will and live like droids, under a new hormonal genetically created human species that cannot do anything that's bad for us. An end to free will, after all, free will doesn't work, does it? What do you think.

This is our time to take what is ours and our future generations from the destructive victims of consumerism and poverty. Education will catch up some day when its finished with technologies attempts to bring us right back where we started. If anyone tried to fix things in the past, they were burnt or shot or hung or genocidically wiped out by industrial consumers, mainly white rich power hungry kings and queens of earthly utopian paradises that are now wracked with the effects of doing wrong. All that they had before them is gone, they are in their graves and their children are suffering the consequences of slavery, colonialism, war, genocide, terrorism...

Who am I? I am Vlad the Impaler, I am Genghis Khan, I am William of Orange, I am Henry the Eighth, I am Hister (Hitler) I am the Irish Chieftain that enslaved English Chieftains and their children during Roman occupation, yes, we started the whole bag of crap in the first place. Who do you think I am? And what does it matter, I am a man, not an animal! Get up off your lazy arses and do something! Stop living like wild sheep, throw away your weaknesses and cop the hell on! For now, just be sure you know where you're going when the lights go out. Weather you're ending it on a high after a last fling, or die in your sleep, remember one thing, somebody somewhere is praying for you. Whatever I did in a past life, I'm dang sure I was somebody, because in this life, I do not give in, I do not stop and I love to feel the power of success. What about you? Are you just another fool? Choosing to listen to your inner critic spell out the waste of energy creativity is and how other people are losers. I think losers are winners, they get to see the rest of us fail. They get to see that opting out gives them a devils right to witness failure and defeat. They become interested in politics when they realize they can represent naïve others. Not all idiots are poor pathetic self absorbed ignorant peasants, are they? Breath in, take a big breath, its all going to be allright, throw away your fears and breath. You've survived this far right? Its helter skelter now isn't it?

CHAPTER FIVE

After a very slow day here in Biarritz followed by the usual spiritual tests, I'm turning to literature to kill the monotony of waiting for a call. Somedays the phone does not ring at all and no customers call to your door. These days I know it's a test and today, so far I have had to endure being stared at by dirty old women whilst going for a swim, it actually made my stomach wretch.

Horror and trauma, I know what its like for young women who are constantly leered at by dirty old or ugly out of shape men. After the swim my landlady calls and says neighbors were complaining about me making noise at night. Well I take calls till 1:00 am, that's it and I'm fairly quiet. They've left anyway, thank god, then after waiting three hours for a call on five different psychic lines, Australia called earlier but that was a freak who told me to "F" off then hung up and called back 4 times. This day so far I've seen a man looking like the devil, with red light coming out the side of his head. Its possible being spiritual is part of the reason why negative energy needs negative or dumb people to connect with. Hey, for those of us in the know, its all good really, when you know you're being tested, it's a little easier, as long as at the end of the week you've made enough to live on, maybe save some, you've beaten the master.

Slavery

Touchy subject, remember, dumb people have to put up with the pressure and stress of their own lives. All problems have to be seen as caused by other people, which to a degree they are, but making things worse is their own fault. Blaming others for everything creates an energy, collectively over half the global population. Energy is God, life-forces of billions of people collectively create one source of light, weather or not they are consciously aware of it, makes no difference. The driving force for consciousness is inherited, its not just instinct we all have, its science too. We have all got a conscience, its helps us decipher mental situations and how we can effect the world through our actions and our thoughts. Seeing spirituality as slavery is a dumb but normal enough attitude to take if it leads the person thinking, so to use this attitude to their advantage. One person will understand that by manipulating believers, or sensitive people their lives will both be easier. The other type uses belief to make money. Selling to both side or both masters, The devil inside and the god inside. Sex sells and creates slaves of us and religion and spirituality sells too. Yoga, meditation classes pay top dollar, statues of Buddha, gold and silver. Trips to Asia, weed and hemp products, save the planet consumerism. Why did indigenous people out hunt certain species or chop down all their trees leading sometimes to self genocide, natures way? Possibly. Are we all slaves? Inside sometimes, maybe. Addiction is a type of slavery, marriage is a type of slavery with the perks of love and honor. Life is a kind of incarceration sometimes isn't it why babies cry when they come out, of the womb? Oh God! I'm here again, but me back! Put me back inside! Bastards! Slaves! Algebra! Dumb humans! Somebody save me!

Thought

The greatest equations will never be known to man (Includes women) We the people includes they the leaders, they too suffer from lifelessness. They too are constantly hounded by their parents, living and passed. They too are forced to be dramatic and seek attention, all their lives. We humans great and small are always being observed. Observed by other people consciously and subconsciously and also observed by our own conscience. Ohh that's a biggee! Conscience.

Should really give that one a heading-conscience! We, as observant people become what is naturally beneficial for us, observation. We are aware of the Id of others. We are always observing the awareness of others, how aware are they, for example? Is their awareness within their own consciousness, or is it from elsewhere, outside of themselves, from another consciousness. From an alien consciousness, such as a jealous aunt or mother. A voice without them. A personality granted the choice to control their siblings throughout their lives. That some of these people are among us and are our own siblings, infected by a situation as old as time itself. "Conspiracy" they conspire towards their goals, their thoughts are based on opposites, the opposite of our thoughts. They have made an unconscious decision to follow the left path of grey knowledge. Listening instead of thinking, why? Because they are born this way, kinda.

These certain types of people feel rejected and only form bonds with others that will help them socially. The greater more positive vibrations of the spirit, to these people, (we are seen as the inferior id.) will form bonds with likeminded others who want revenge on the world, that's what they think is the meaning of life. Take all that you see before you. Sensitive people will "give" them safe passage through life. Life is a game, so why not play by their own rules-Hitler did. White people did when they killed Aborigines, Native Americans, Irish peasants, English peasants, French peasants, Basque Nationals, Jews, Romans, Carthaginians, Sumerians, Bavarians, Italians. Fascism is among us, it's a natural part of our families. Our society, our music and culture, our thought processes. It generates gold for the system, without pain we wouldn't need medicine, healers, witches, wizards, and war.

Angels belong on Earth.

We were meant to be idealistic (Pun) We are idealistic, fact. We choose to be, or not to be. We are lucky or unlucky, some of the time. We are single, we are free, we experiment with our soul body or not. We are sensitive, or not. We are controlled by our free will or not. Controlled? Ok, We are allowed to think for ourselves. We are allowed to study angels or angelic magic or witchcraft. We are becoming recognized by other angelic beings and healers as healers with experience, with ability and with the capacity to survive all onslaughts and addictions. Including sexual addiction, nicotine, alcohol, sugar, coffee, anger, blame, ignorance, fear, the list is endless. Our role in the world now is to help people to survive. To re-learn the craft of our ancestors. To survive in the process without being "Recruited" by the soul experimentation movement or the anti experimentation movement. Angels are possessed with power, or they possess power, we are not angels. Some of us can attain angelic power, but only through discipline, discipline that usually includes experimentation. This new millennium is a time for all young and old to embrace the light. To become one with the light, or become lost in the darkness. There are spirits amongst us, as there always have been. These spirits are known to all human beings. Some of us veer away from listening to what's around us and concentrate on normality. Even these people are unconscious of their own subconscious thoughts that are constantly communicating with spirits and ancestors and god knows, probably the whole spectrum of spiritual manifestation. Angels are at the top of the heap, they rule over certain kingdoms if you will. Earth and air, fire and water spirits are also about.

Birth

We are born, we live, we die. I prefer to use the word, reborn rather than die. We are on a plane, of existence, always have been, for a good while anyway. When we enter this earthly plane, we go through a metamorphosis that brings us back to where we came from, eventually, originally. In the meantime we re-enter the world as our good old selves as we were and always have been from our past lives as, women, men or animals, or plants even. The wisdom we accumulate as these eons pass, give us insight into ourselves and other people, nature and our paths, around this earth. Chinese in one life, Tibetan in another, Royal genocidal maniac in one life, Irish freedom fighter in another. Its to teach us that choice is either personal or preferred, like national pressure to conform to idealistic beliefs such as communism and its failings, or fascism and its failings, or capitalism and its compromises. Compromising a new era, giving "Birth" to new ides, ideas of individual freedom and then taking it all away by telling us that were all guilty of killing the planet. Well give me five minute to live my life first and see how much recycling I'm responsible for, wait a minute, were already doing that. Or at least some trash man conglomerate is making millions from recycling, so I'm off the hook right? What about the sea levels rising or eating animal protein? Isn't this also wrong? Drinking alcohol (I don't) isn't this wrong? Smoking, well this is on the way out, or is it? Are we still playing God by being told what were supposed to be thinking. In the meantime some people are happy to just say sod it, I'm off to the pub for a pint of stout, a cigar and a beef casserole, so what! Others say I'm off to the gym for some yoga and a tofu filled hash cookie, so what! Gyms cost water to build, there's a problem, water is now another problem in capitalism, it takes so much water to make a fork, a knife, a plastic bowl, do you see any naturistic enthusiasts making their own utensils to save the Planet? Some are growing their own food, making their own knives and forks, god knows what else. Some people are opting out of carbon emissions completely, well as much as is humanly possible. Making their own clothes, growing their own food, and still dyeing of cancer from smoking their own weed (Hashish-skunkweed, ecstasy e.t.c.) They're not hypocrites, are they? Who am I to judge.

Rebirth

Tell you the truth I'm only writing now to spite the machine. The energy controlling my life and yours, in contempt for the race that ignores the delicate balance between right and wrong. It could become a national pastime to be belligerent, in some countries, like it already is (Pun) pun, that's a joke, I think, absolutely. Belligerence comes from being born into a society with a chip on its shoulder, a collective self image of, eh, people with attitude. Where personalities run short on individualism and self realization. Where there's a feeling that control is normal, or a good thing. Where religion allows losers to follow their expected potential of, live, drink, work, sex, drink, work, marriage, drink, eat, love and hate, tattoos of love and hate, football, every day, white trash fashion and babies with skinheads. It's a judgment on belligerence and who came blame them? After all they were born to lose and made to sin. The media told them to do it, honest! The bars and publicans had to make way or else! Bigger pubs, more pubs, more "Offies" more drugs, more sex, more booze, follow the fashion, you'll never walk alone. We all go down together. Its all good, live and let live, only they don't like people who do. It stands to reason that in this lifetime, we the people are beset upon by a number of factors. Karma, what our ancestors did to their ancestors is the reason they are idiots in this lifetime. Their forefathers were picked on by ours. Innocent victims of ignorance and greed by our ancestors has lead to us and ours being beset upon by the inheritors of pain and poverty in pocket and in spirit. Not to get political (Impossible) Our ancestors killed Native Americans, Aborigines, enslaved Africans e.t.c. We did it dressed in the red coat uniforms of the people that killed us like animals and made us live like animals. Innocent people were destroyed by our greedy serving the crowns genocidal anti Christ ancestors. So in this lifetime we have to pay, it makes perfect sense doesn't it, you would think. That's not fair I hear you say, your not the first people to say this. It shouldn't matter what my great, great uncles or aunts did, it should, it does, it is. So the next time somebody mugs or harasses you, just remember, its karma. Inescapable karma, or effect if karma is a culture-shock for your psyche. I expect most of you know what a psyche is, or culture shock, after all you did learn to read, you did go to school. Didn't you? We all came from the same place more or less. Were all going back there just not the way we came in. Ultimately, when we do arrive at where we left off, there's going to be somebody waiting, for us, when we get there.

Who's waiting for us here? Whose interested in our journey now? Enemies from a past life, revenge fuelled haters wanting to vent frustration on us little innocents, mostly as karma for where our minds are at most of the time. How many times a day do you think of chemical love for example? And why do you? Spirits make you, other peoples spirits, your spirits, Earth, Air, Fire and Water spirits, many, many spirits do. Why wouldn't they? Primal forces driving primal survival mechanisms that drives the people on. Fearless of responsibility, naïve to the point of idiocy and beyond! Eat, drink and be merry for tomorrow we may have to face the consequence. Well tomorrow is here. Millennium is here, where are you? Here? No. You think you're here, you're there, on the other side, don't you remember? That bump on the head you never saw coming? Oh, yea, tip the hat and scratch your head, maybe. No maybes about it mate, you've been over on the flip-side for the amount of time it took you to read this, right here, right now, years of living somewhere else, do you feel like you're living in someone else's body? Perhaps. Someone else's imagination? Is that what heaven is? Ahem, you're interested in heaven now? But what about the meaningless blonde bimbo? Right! Perhaps she is a sign of your appetite for testing yourself, do you have a daughter? That blond you see out there every day, is she old enough to be your daughter, can you look at her as if she is? Respect yourself mate, respect the youth and grow up or be gone.

God? He was only a figment of your imaginary existence, perhaps you are imaginary, maybe this whole world is, it could be for you, it could be. Decide.

Headers, Nutbags and Fruits.

Constance will flow through all stops, anything that keeps us going. More and more we remember our history and decide to act upon our choice. For the first time in your life, you choose, to think, for yourself. When was the first time? When you decided you couldn't afford to drink that night and went out dancing anyway, had a great time after dancing all night and knew that there was goodness in it. No hangover, no connection to the other people either, who were drinking. Moderation found you 20 years later avoiding the point and eventually you had to stop drinking because you became sick or addicted. Now you "Think" before you enter a pub. I wont drink anymore because…the list is endless. I wont smoke because I'm sick, or have cancer. You're getting older, mid 40s, you're a little out of shape, losing some teeth, hair thinning, people laugh louder when your around. What's up with that? (Wouldn't you like to know) Midlife crisis! It's the best thing that ever happens to us all. We remember those old men laughing at our youthful fearlessness, in their knowledge of life, they know well what's in store for us, failure, pain and ignorance. Boom! Impotence, baldness, fat, jowls, ill health, weakness in the joints, emotional imbalance, mental sensitivity or nerves…it goes on. We try to change things, go jogging, eat less crap, it makes a difference. So, what's all the fuss? You're in your 40s, your "OK" things are allright, people who laugh are always fatter and dumber anyway, congratulations you've survived, now what?

Life begins, that's what, welcome to adulthood, welcome to choice. Choice is our first experience with memory. Its elemental Watson, your human. Choosing not to flirt, that's the hardest thing to do, you've now got to re-learn everything you've taken for granted all your stupid life! How to communicate. Becoming an adult is like re-learning how to talk after having a stroke. How not to look at younger people because you're "Horney" how to live in a respectful way towards others, others that despise respect because they've never had it, never. Suddenly, things are different, your waking up, to a new world, its an adventure. Were not alone in this world, of course we always have the non-believers.

And what of them, they call me all the time, I deal with them my own special way, I compliment the cause of their ailment. Whilst I write, there are always spirits around me, struggling to effect my words, threatening terrible consequences if I don't listen to them. Manifesting in the bodies of local idiots, winos, perverts, spasticated nimrods, assholes and imbeciles. Forgive my foul language but I'm only human. No offense to special or challenged people, they know what I'm talking about right? They live in a world full of idiots that call themselves normal.

Qualified Dysfunction

Dysfunction is the meaning of life. Being dysfunctional is perfection of a sort, it allows us to always be ready for more, always look forward to better things. We feel like something is watching over us when we are too busy to be bored or tired, when were active, working, full of energy. So, when were tired of life, or people or were angry at some idiot for putting us into a rage, its because we were in need of energy. We needed to feel alive, so negative energy helped us to give us drive, to achieve some dramatic calamity to keep us occupied in the meantime.

What! Why! Where! Who! I hear you say, why? Why not, why not have something crazy happen to give us a burst of hormones and adrenalin in a world where we used to get these chemicals every day. In war, hunting, running e.t.c. Running is one of the most exciting sports out there, but many of us think, Oh I'm too tired for that, ill stick with pacing myself through life. Ill go to the gym, later, or ill get lucky on the weekend and that will be my burst of hormonal high. Or ill get unlucky with some local who freaks me out and will play on my mind so much I worry myself into a paranoid flutter.

True victims of oppression do it all the time. Ever wonder why some people go crazy on CNN. News when their child has been shot? Holding their hands up to their heads and screaming for God? Oh God, help me! Well its usually because their child has just been murdered.

But for the people who don't have real problems, it just a booze fuelled freak-out! Oh Jesus! God! God! AAAAGGGGHHHH! Its their way of getting some free hormones. Not getting paid enough or being bullied out of your home by colonial forces, pick up a gun and kill somebody, get energized! Kill or be killed, fight or flight, that's the way of the world. Oh, chill man, Ill do some yoga then get lucky, that's a cop out, save the planet then get laid, it's a losers game.

Somewhere out there, are people who are powerful in a greater way than local fear and primal forces. Somewhere out there are successful people, living successfully, through hell and high water, literally. Burning desires to feel free, to be good at something, so much so that they are recognized as such. Artists, politicians that everybody ridicules yet secretly wants to be, if they cant, they can always control the rest of us via petty jealousy and mind games. Mind games are political. Politics at its base level, you me and the imp that carries thoughts of antagonism and envy.

The origin of God

Every time I use words, a spirit to my left tells me not to say them, what's happening is, the spirit that's telling me to use words is constructive , also to the left, the left path(Generally) and good or benevolent. The spirit that's telling me not to, is negative or conflicted and restless, it's the inner critic, the anti-muse. Some people believe that God is just a voice in out heads, a collective energy that represents benevolence. Did we create god or did god create us? Well before you ask that, study the origin of Gods. The origin of Gods is man-woman-child e.t.c. Or life, male-female offspring. It's a force, a life force, the beginning of things, amoeba to identity.

Existence is fraught with politics, life verses anti-life. Death isn't the opposite of life, its just the absence of life, physical life, cell-life. Spirit lives before and after cell-life. Metaphorical cell-life can feel like a slow death, I'm living in a cell, I feel imprisoned and fenced in e.t.c. It can lead to death through depression, it even has a religion-like addiction of woe be tide attitudes for people who worship negative analytical attitudes. These people are a political force that objects to positive thinking. They tried it, it didn't work, so like a wheel in the hands of a pre-caveman, they rejected it. Let someone else do the thinking, I'm ignorant, its bliss. Politics is for the stupid educated folk. Non-educated folk are just as intelligent as academics, they've just educated themselves, by deduction. Its deduction that invented the wheel, the first utensils for making things, the first objects that represent life, or divine invention. Blades help to see within, they represent the mind. Bowls help to hold things, especially water, this represents emotion or "Soul". Stones for crushing wheat, or other peoples heads, represent earth and physical power. Staffs represent fire, for burning or supporting earth in the air as arrows or spearheads or axe handles.

Think for yourself, come up with your own ideas for life and its origins of beliefs and thought provoking creation and creations.

Right now, here and now, some of you will have been affected by this last paragraph. Powerful forces in your lives, right now! Here and now! I would love to know how you changed your life because of your understanding of what has just happened, how you will learn that power is organic and is always waiting. Waiting for you, every day of your life. Run! Run like the wind! Feel the fire within as your energy soars like an eagle, as your heart pounds like a stag in full flight. Boom, boom, boom, boom, your heart beats and you feel alive! Run fast and free, then stretch and shower and chill, if you can. Feel it on your face as you swim in the sea in mid-winter, that glow that is irrepressible, you'll even begin to feel good about all challenges and rest when everything is in its place. Oh, yes, its good to feel alive, even when your body is no more. Especially then.

Headless Corpses

How's that for a header! I Went to visit one of Napoleon Bonaparte's wives houses last night, its just down the road from me. On an almost full Moon, two days before Halloween in Biarritz. There's a good vibe there, it's a palace of a home, with designs beneath the windows as buttresses or something. As a medium I see things on a very subtle level, that's hard to accept at first, most of you have this ability, it comes with being a person. I could tune in sometimes and ask the spirit to show me something but a lot of the time spirits are bursting to show themselves anyway. I saw on this occasion, a person losing their head, God bless them, It just fell off their shoulders, ahh, poor baby. That same night as I was going to bed they appeared before me just as I was putting my own sweet little head down to rest. It was very scary and very different from anything I've ever encountered. She was also strangely enough attracted to me, it helped in my rapport with her. I asked her to be friendly and also looked around the room afterwards to remind myself that she was gone and it was partly a trick of the mind (I hoped) You see, because you can see them, they know it, and they like to make contact, communicate, even play games. All psychics have that little voice in their ear telling them its not real, or your not psychic and your inner child is really not a good little boy or girl after all.

We have to register that in our world the general population are brainwashed by conformist philosophies and anybody interested in freedom of thought is hounded out of normal society. You'll never be published if you write the truth! You'll end up in a mental asylum, why? Because that's where these little voices experiences placed people like you and me in the past. One of the last houses I lived in was beside an old hospital that subscribed lobotomies for psychic people and mentally or spiritually disturbed people, thinking they were skitzo. These " Little voices" that hound us, or try to, can be controlled, or bound and banished, but its an eternal process of clearing. Most of us ignore weird mental stuff, its just our brains acting stressed or bored or whatever. Its a very subtle world we live in and subtle doesn't mean weak or ineffectual, it means hidden, secretive, controlling, this means emotional trouble sometimes. The thoughts that rule many idiots are subtle manifestations of fear, fear of being judged by others, also the realization or anti-realization that these "Thoughts" are helping them, they are. Helping to possess some people with spirits of control, from the micro to the macro worlds. Heedlessness is their problem, make sure you remember this, because it's a plague on humanity that thought can lead to some people losing their heads.

Obviously, if you are an alcoholic, tired and down, your thoughts will be negative and may even seem to turn on you and start attacking you and calling you names. Get help. The rest of us, keep our minds clear by thinking and that's keeping the mind occupied. This also leads to blabbing inside and breathing is the key to slowing down the mind and allowing for mental peace.

Flowing

Stream of consciousness, used to love it, still do, going with the flow as far as it takes you. Listening to the heads around me, bizarre as they may seem gives us a clear impression of collective consciousness. Heads are banging off dashboards as we speak, they're on their way out and down that road as fast as they can just to avoid the catastrophe of thought. Thoughtlessness is better than facing the results of emotional fact. Fact is fact for some, fiction for others. It all depends on how your week is going, month, year, lifetime, lifetimes. I just realized my head is always full of what's going on around me. Who's passing by, what's up with the rest of the world, what's going on inside the heads of the people id rather like to know. Who's in this world now that isn't a celebrity, that isn't an amateur know it all catastrophe theorist.

Don't want to know them, just want to know the cool people, the really cool people. Hermitage is a metaphor, many of us live and work alone because the people around us aren't real people, they're empty shallow, lost souls seeking truth in our reality. Alien space invaders lost in a world of their own, a meaningless world of idiocy and waste. The world of the fly, the weak low vibration characters world. Believe me, all people have something to give, we all play a role, were all in the right place, not always at the right time. Go with it, role with it, be one with your serendipity, give good times a chance again, get out there. Go dancing, even put on some music and dance at home, just get energized somehow, its all in your head. People come to me all day, every day, even when its just the need of locals, they're still looking for attention.

I tell them what they need to know, about why their partner isn't able to support them, its because their partner has a mother complex, or a Casanova complex e.t.c When they leave their homes their problems follow them, for some reason the Universe is following them with problems until they deal with them. We all have problems and we all have to deal with them, but how? How does a man or woman deal with the problems other people bring into their lives? Magic spells? Yes! Prayer? Yes! Philosophy, meditation, positive thinking that's how. Even people with complexes can overcome them, its all about self realization and the long and winding road home. Were all born self realized, awake, open minded, ready for new experiences, each and every one of us, we all have brains in our heads.

Self realization

Prostitution of the soul, for many of those who seek to better themselves. Open your mind and your ass will follow, just ask any man that's tried yoga. The route to perfection always takes the slow road of experience, its natural, why not just go with the flow. Buda experienced everything, and I mean everything that you're not meant to try, freak show mumbo jumbo magic mushroom hallucinating tongue dropping drugs and starvation techniques, you name it he tried it. Is it possible were all on the same path of self discovery, even if we don't want to be.

G-spot routes to an anal end, joys of the physical body, all types of sexuality to Pan-sexuality for many seeking the oneness with the Divine is all part and parcel of the pseudo modernistic approach to spiritual experimentation. Wow! If only I was born in the 60s! I was, but only just, the tail of the snake, Paganism has arrived, lock up your daughters and certainly don't send them to the void, they will be requited into the hermaphroditic-hood! All puns aside, forgiveness please. Many spiritual saints were supposedly hounded by demons, vying their trades upon the sensitive souls pertaining towards a spiritual existence, i.e. they were human and so susceptible to sexual desires outside of their own, i.e. ignoramus, local hero's and heroines, vessels of succubus and concubine.

Why you didn't think women would be excluded, did you? Its not an exclusive club you know, the blame game. We've all been brainwashed into thinking along these lines, male-female. One world ruled by one law, another ruled by another. Its all good, it is really. Oh those kids these days will try anything, Sex is sugar, alcohol is sugar, drugs are sugar, yes even sugar is. Is sugar a euphemism, that's a rhetorical question, you know I'm speaking metaphorically don't you? Ahem, be careful.

Soullessness is part of the journey of discovery, as long as experience is around. We, consumers are born into an anachronised world that's ruled by chaos, that in turn was created by the failure of diplomacy and tact, i.e. Fundamentalistic approaches to rule. You and me, our forefathers were ruled by tax collecting vampires, within the body of collective mental extremism. They lost their heads… We are here now to watch opportunists save the planet. Some crazy hippies started something back in the 80s and some consumer got their grubby paws on it, now we have recycling. Big money, making poor people rich, my oh my, the banks really do help the little guys, don't they! Meanwhile all the save The Earth people are smoking themselves to death on supergrass. Not cool, and impotent metaphorically. Next you'll have religions based upon the control of the devil-worshipping public telling them the parties over. Well maybe that's a job for the spirit-world, they're very accommodating over there when it comes to poor little prostituted drug-overdosed party animals who've finished with their blamelessness and have opted out for Winterland. Ah yes, where the Moon is always shinning and the rivers are made of booze and the grass really is smokable, and everybody wants to party, non-stop for all eternity, great…don't worry, someone else will clean up after you and make a fortune reselling it back to you at thrice the price. We made it! We stuck together as a whole and supported each other when nobody else wanted to. Those damned consumers!

Plastic empty vessels eating pork and other domesticated animals conforming to a whole other network of fascist ideology. I did what I was told! I revolted against conformity, I blamed the right people right? Didn't you just, you blamed the people on the opposing team, the people with cars and mortgages, and college funds, people like your parents, who worked and toiled for your college fund, who paid taxes that funded you social welfare for 40 years and paid for your free council house. Great! Its all good…next life I can come back and thank everyone for working for me as I devoted myself to saving trees planted by the slave-masters 400 years ago. Oak trees, sacred oak tree planted by the lord and lady of Doncaster, paid for in blood diamonds and planted by Irish paupers in Wicklow for better hunting of quail and pheasant. Great, yea, save those trees why don't you. Glen of the Downs, looking more like the forest from the "Wizard of OZ." Destruction, anarchy, debauchism, why? Consumerism destroyed Druids and Earth Religion the World over, that's why.

Holy- Prostitute

The world doesn't thank them, you know. Mary Magdalene, I'm sure started life an idealistic child of upper-class parents, set out to prove her equality to the ordinary folk. She wanted to be like other people, wanted to sleep with other people, wanted to embrace some form of love in a love-less world, why not start by loving everyone. Then the Universe steeped in to "Test" her, poor misguided baby. Hashish probably lead to stronger drugs, i.e. Opium. Strange spirits entered her life when she hit 18 and then some. Boom! The world in all its glory began to push her away from the love of the people, into a world of sexual experimentation.

While Budda was off hitting the highs and lows of Alchemical discipline, it was her turn to see what the world really wants from sensitive souls. Servitude. Like all sensitive people, we must either serve the divine, or serve the anti-divine and dine on that for a while. A serving of both for the Libran-Gemini in us all, until life has punished us enough for being more animal-human than human in the body. She immersed herself into the life of politicians, she slept with the enemy, the meta-phorical rat, the dog, the cat, the frog. The weasel and the toad, all asunder, she knew the wisdom of the fool, the joker, the madman and the lord. All men (some Women) were sedated by the beast within, made animals of themselves and were sedated. Good people all of them, pillars of the under-world society that supports their opposites, extreme fundamentalists. She was the whore with the heart of gold, she was a hedonistic saint a Goddess, a powerful master of men, she made mountains move, made prophets famous, she was their labyrinthian Muse, their Lilithian Aphrodite. Then the walls came crashing down

When the legend met the facts, she started to fall, she couldn't live up to the expectations of all, there began to appear cracks in the armor. Oh no! Don't shatter the dream, don't take the power of sedatives away from us, we will punish you, collectively. Don't you feel the pain of our lives driving us to entertainment and revelry, its our human right! You should never get between a dog and its dinner.

She slowly started to suffer. Disease became "Normal", her reputation as queen of the harem started to wane, when her beauty began to fade, her domain became one of sloth and addiction. Some people even started to want her place in the world of power and influence, some wanted her head, or worse. There were evil beings around, stirring in the ether, waiting for something, someone special. Time had found its place and a dark power laid in waiting for a new era to begin, but what, and with whom? Know one really knew, they had forgotten the impotence of prophesy, they had learned about the "Grey" world of men, the world of joy, indulgence and temperance. A balance, where all is good. All is to be celebrated, "Health!" they will say, and health they will lose, its ironic. (If you understand irony)

Dramatic? Yes, indeed, but it a grey world out there and we love our little dramas, all the world and all its little players. Bigger pictures usually attract bigger people, both physically and metaphysic-ally. Playing God, usually ends up with becoming, old and frail just like peasant-like middle class voters do, its helps prepare the soul for weighing and measuring. We will always have a struggle be-tween life and anti-life, there is no struggle between life and death, why would there be?

Every fool loves to endorse their peers, they have to, to fit in with them. Fools and jokers spend all their waking hours selling truthisms and rejecting truthisms. As an artist I have to listen to their cries for attention and sickness and adulterous self-indulgent indolence because their cries are loud and cannot be ignored. Its all a plea for attention from attention deficit disordered mobs with spiritual A.S.B.O.s on their tails (pun) Its not their faults, poor devils, they were badly treated by society, or their mothers, somebody's always to blame. Ironically, many the boozed out, smoked out rebels wear crucifixes and prey to their favorite saints for love and protection. There is good in louts after all. We could all end up being one, if were not careful, to our enemies, we will always be to epitome of failure, shame and self depreciation, ah, the spirits are with them, don't you think they're not.

Demonically possessed imbeciles

Its true, I'm regressing, but when you think of it, that's the meaning of life, open your mind, then live in isolation ask any single talk show host, its true. For years now I have tried and been tested, I tried to figure it all out. Once and a while the Gob****** left me alone just long enough to suffer righteously, or at least they thought it was their idea. That's another meaning of life, that ass ****s think they think at all, Idiots don't think, remember, they listen. Little Devils seem to be moving into my Headspace ever since the supposed return of Christ in 2000.

Id be a hypocrite if I didn't ask "God" for forgiveness, please forgive me Lord. All a sundry is riddling my brain for space these days, it almost feels like the end is nigh for half The Earths population of thick-numbskulls. If I didn't want revenge on the world more than making a living from it I would have tossed myself into Hell years ago (Pun) In fact just yesterday I told one of my customers to perform a metaphorical act on me!

Its impossible to beat a demon in a conversation, but oh Man I'm getting better at it all the time. All is vanity, so they say, no I didn't mean I wanted her to, it was a metaphor, a metaphor, you do know what a metaphor is don't you, no don't Google it moron just get off my book! Its all wonderful, I'm working six jobs and still not earning any money, but don't worry, I've got another three in the pipeline. It couldn't be my fault, I'm doing everything right. Any Psychic worth their salt knows what I'm going through, some white Trash Ass**** calls you, you do your best, but soul destroying demons do exist and they know how to get to you, for Christ's sake, has someone turned out the lights?

Butterflies do fart and people do die, some of them need to, they have pushed too far. We have all unwittingly been attached to certain thoughts in our lives, I wouldn't blame anybody for wanting to end the life of someone who pushed them over the edge, it happens, all the time. Murder most foul. Were here, and yes we can! Was that sentence too close to the other sentence? Should I have moved it somewhere else, people can get ideas y `know. Life springs eternal for all the little Hitler's out there, Run! Run into the streets and fly high into the abyss of Gods forgiveness, take advantage of sensitive privileged middle class people, their weak and they deserve it, use your ethnicity as an excuse, or perhaps your demons undying love for sex and alcohol, its all good, Bam! Bam! Bam! Shot through the head, who can blame you, I don't. Honestly, God knows you, he knows you have a threshold for being the scapegoat for losers reason to be an Ass****, look it up in the little Book of terrorism "Thouest where born from an Ass, thouest shall live as one" And they do.

Anti-depressants, I will never do them (Liar) Oh you naïve little souls, so naïve, so strong, so able to take the brunt. How you doin now in 20?? eh? Not so easy now with Big Bertha or whatever metaphorical storm in a teacups coming down on you like a Hell Whores day off, and on your case (May all the Whores of Hell please, forgive me) They weren't loved as children, they deserve to punish the rest of us, we deserve to put up with eternal woe from scumbags and perverts. Hey, it's the meaning of life, have a nice day!

I'm turning into Beetlejuice! Well its how I entered adolescence. Manhood now expresses itself with a new gusto ever since I entered a country where woman are allowed to be women. Equality doesn't seem to be such a big issue in European first world countries. They have always been very futuristic regarding women's place in society is super feminine yet still powerful and intelligent. Recovering third world countries values seem retarded compared to attitudes based on what the rest of the world may be doing. Its ok to criticize basically.

There is a need for all of us to see media values as directions for collective ideals. People who play God and Goddess in our world, we criticize the need for them, Politicians, Clergy (Anachronism?) Police States e.t.c. We criticize and begin to blame everybody but our complacent selves. Sexual choices too are under constant surveillance by our peers. People who experiment are instantly labeled "Danger areas" by heterosexuals and same sex experimentation alike. We are full of hypocrisy and bigotry towards each other. Consumers secretly hoard personal political persuasions as dreams and fantasies, let the actual Politicians do the grubby work of pretend work as the voters do all the real work.

Consumers don't know anything about politics which is why all they do is talk about it on Facebook. Communists aren't allowed to voice their opinions, socialists spend all their time as philanthropists and Anarchists are recovering in Re-hab on a drip, or in a prison cell. Is experimentation regarded as free will? Is this a war on creativity in a world gone mad for what the man at the top allows us to purchase-pulp!

Multi millionaires control our thoughts when they control the choices available to us. Since the first supermarkets slipped in to our city streets in the 70s we have belonged to one type or another, quality or quantity. Religion also fits into this categorization of personal choices. Mass or meditation, conformity or revolutionary. Revolutionaries are outcasts, vegetarians are outcasts, bisexuals are outcasts, asexuals are seen as non-threatening people with Messiah complexes. Our consumers are building a collective consciousness and don't even know it, the middle class mostly.

The people who pay most in taxes, buy the best cars available and affordable, go to the best schools and colleges. Eat, drink and multiply with balanced regularity, the perfection of the Human Race is the creation of the modern middle class. Hollywood makes movies about them, happy, poetic inspired beings full of potential. A wonderful life. The creation of royalty in origin, those whom serve the kings and queens as dukes and earls and chieftains. Powerful people who represent morally educated constructive tribal elders. Our Planet has plenty of able beings, full of hope for a better future, constructing a modern world that functions better and with more respect for nature than any community that has come before. Why? We are environmentally aware, of over fishing, waste disposal, air pollution, toxic waste. We are educated by the media only as entertainment. We vote to protect ourselves from the wrong leadership destroying what constructive people have created. New world order is, weather we like it or not, inevitable. It is happening in Europe, it will happen elsewhere, Mother Africa is aware of our existence and very interested in saving herself from pollution and genocide. She saw what was coming and watched as her children were snatched from her arms into the new world as one road to self sacrifice leading out of perdition. This is Apocalypse, some of us are ready for the new dawn, some of us are sadly, on the blame game and are not ready at all.

Intensity of literary skill, too many words as one secretary complained about having to type for me, even though she lost all of my work. This is just another planet, trying to get to grips with flying whilst still anchored to the earthly plane. Some of us are constant in the fight for more than before. Bigger, better, faster, safer, cleaner, everybody else just takes what they're given and does their best with it.

We are not chosen by God, none of us, that's a cop out, we choose to be able for the job though. Also being aware means listening to both sides of the story at the same time. If there are people who worship negative thoughts around us, we must have an eye on the fly attitude towards them. They are cursed in many ways by their own idiocy, its political. Many of these people are relatives, many of them are friends, or old friends, or old enemies, or ethnic minorities that view you as privileged and the cause of all of their suffering. Criminal, isn't it. Sic Semper Tyrannis!

I have noticed, the more we have, the less we appreciate it. We begin to understand what's more important than things, money, survival, existence, health e.t.c. Ambition, is more important then survival, animals survive, some humans too, but for us, the modern beings in an ever increasingly accessible world, more than before is possible without greed or destruction.

Climbing to metaphysical heights. Getting through the energies of daily tasks and low vibration energies to achieve great energies. With the help of herbal remedies of course. Take your royal jelly and your rhodiola, and live temperately and with moral discipline and this Millennium is an adventure. When your winning dance! It may only last a moment, it feels like being in love. Energy, energy is what the modern world is obsessed with, generators, nuclear power, electricity, all these things are manifestations of spiritual forces. Industrialization destroyed all organic forms of energy as much as it could. Why? Because of one mans greed for power and self importance, the rich man and his wife. Men used to represent all that was good about society. Women on the other hand used to be repressed and could have represented all that was good about modern society, do they? Maybe the selling point for freedom does.

Were all drones for the greater destiny of mankind, person-kind. Children-kind will be the generation that experiences a 1,000 years of freedom and an eventual One World Order. Before aliens try to invade (Perhaps)

Our minds are constantly fed with energy, the energy of thought. What's coming next, how, where, why, whom and with what? We need to stop thinking and meditate, exercise, get up off the couch and walk, run, swim ourselves out of our heads and live a little. Millennium is all about life, living, moving forwards, giving energy back to the world. Experiencing living things, weather your fit or not, this year will be challenging our recourses macro and micro. Petrol is too expensive, pretty soon we wont be able to afford our own Funerals.

Wont be able to afford war or peace. Might as well live for the moment, ignorance is still bliss. No matter what you read in the papers, or see and hear on TV. the world will continue on without us. There is another television, another media, the real media of good people, people with good energy, exciting people, wonderful people, beautiful inside people with energy to give, boundless energy. A god king or queen will give up on gold and feed her people, build houses for the poor, feed the hungry, Tax less the middle people and live for the future. Our politicians earn 500,000 a year, why? I don't know. Some of these big earners have the gaul to call themselves socialists, what's social about that. What was the first thing The American President did? Fire and re-hire. Reduce the wages of overpaid staff and let go of fearful scare mongering tactics. Ignoring a problem doesn't make it go away, it just gives us a rest from listening to lies. All politicians are actors, when will we ever learn that democracy is just as evil as communism, just nit as retarded in its beliefs. Leave the Tibetans alone you nimrods!

If scientists ruled to world, all we would have would be lies. There is no God, all is motion, motion is physics, not spirit, energy is scientific not spiritual. We would be living a genetically modified existence where scientists would block out the sun, and charge us for the privilege.

Popular Messiah

For each genre, there is a messiah, chosen by the mogul, the person at the top. The person who rules the roost, who chooses what poet or painter makes it to the top of their peer group. Psychic editing is a cancer, it is a bacteria that infects our minds, we are being edited by the machine. Organic money orientated machine, compromising our convictions for inevitable revelations. gold. Gold is the prize physically and metaphysically. We are winners after all, we hope our gold comes from fair trade and is mined within our countries, if we belong to any country. We watch movies about freedom, created by artists that are under scrutiny from their governments, especially in America. Communism was under investigation within Hollywood a few decades ago and probably still is. We love our little spy in the ointment routine, just ask neighbors what they think. They secretly think we threaten their existence, were a strange bunch of conspiracy theorists us suburbians.

Keep it consumer friendly, but Avant Garde all the same, you Commies! Nuclear War is imminent! Build you walls higher! metaphysical walls that is. Three month holiday visa? No problem! Come and visit, come and see, it's a beautiful place, were proud of it, its all world famous! Come eat the world famous hot dogs, pizza, visit New York and see the miles and miles of poverty stricken venders selling woolen socks and army and navy hats and gloves in downtown Manhattan. Its amazing!

World famous woolen gloves for $5. Wow! I've got to go there, its wonderful! Yea! Wow! Awesome! Get as far away from communists as I can, scumbags, maybe I can get a little stall and be like the people in the movies and sell my soul in Time Square! Wow! Awesome!

Modern messiahs sell what we need back to us. What we lack in our personal lives. They give it to us freely via the media. Name that will not be mentioned, selling number one hits about love and freedom. He "Really" cares. Its getting better and better. The machine allows him to sell the idea of freedom to sedate us, the masses, that's what we are.

Books about magick and empowerment are a one way route to success, its guaranteed! As long as you chase the buck, anything could, and does happen. I'm selling right now and your buying! Sell, sell, buy, buy! It's a revolution!

Momentum, energy, freedom, back to work on Monday, unless your on the dole for life. I could have been. Truth is for sale, it comes with a bar code, it gives artists freedom to create. Don't "fund it" that's begging, were not beggars were revolutionaries. Arnt we? Non-mentionable name, was a rebel, a revolutionary, he fought the system, he told us how it was, how it is, his memory will cost 1,000 lives 10,000 lives in the name of freedom(sex, drugs and stupidity). Buy his books, listen to his music.

Another non-mentionable name, the famous revolutionary, buy his T-Shirts for the cause, smoke cigars and take cocaine, get pissed and scream revolution! Forgive me all of you famous messiahs, I don't mean any harm, I'm just selling my ideas to my fans, my clients, perhaps they will build a statue of me someday and I will be reveled as the artist revolutionary of the millennium, born in the 60s.

Modern day messiahs sell fame to you, Joe public. X Factor, queue up Factor, 15 mins of total world domination and then millions of people start thinking "What about me?" You can be famous too, never stop believing. Never take that poster down from the wall, worship eternally. Love it! Its all good and its all for sale, unless your giving it away for free. Do you spend your time singing in the workplace? Do people tell you have a beautiful voice? Are you always dreaming of being loved by many and adored by 1,000s? You can!

Its true, you can, if you work hard, baloney? Work and practice and take lessons and learn by experience what its all about, then when you're ready, sell! But get an agent first, forget about self advertisement, that's for bums. (No offence)

Pretty much what happens when half the world sells back our messiahs to us when its done with them via documentaries on their murder or suicide or death by misadventure hanging from a doorframe by your belt buckle with a smile on your face, when their in spirit, getting stoned immaculate, flies into an abyss, like only famous people who lose their sparkle can. In the name of all spirits, forgive me, I am the one who will set your spirit free. For a price.

Who sells these stories, well their agents or their families, after all sibling rivalry was the origin of all evil in their formation years, it stands to reason they should own the rights to the life stories of their famous children. Things are changing and these days there is more moral obligation after the fact, to support charities and educate young people on the dangers of alcohol consumption and immorality. Perhaps the sacrifices made by world famous artists are a saintly act, if even as an oxymoron. (No offence)

Kill or be killed, swing or be swung, sell or be sold, worship or be worshipped, run or be run down, create or be entertained. The audience will always lap it up, always buy the latest product for Christmas, this isn't a planet, it's a business.

Unless you're a really good Christian, then all you have to do is avoid dreams, live the nightmare and wait for a good clean death before you achieve anything.

No one person dies in vain, they all serve a purpose, years of trial and error, building a safe haven for future generations, ready to overcome all incurable illnesses. Who creates incurable illnesses? we do.

Inconsequential Evidence

The meaning of life? Two choices, selfishness or selflessness? Somewhere in between. Double standards, ethics, politics (Personal politics) socks with sandals? Sometimes. Meat? Sometimes. Dairy? All of the time. Equality? Blah, blah, blah e.t.c.

On it goes, never stopping, life. Constant, forever, eternal, whatever your beliefs. Work, is the key to survival. Retired people find themselves without a purpose and swiftly dwindle. Peaceful people are in the same boat, drifting down endless sunny pavilions, bored beyond belief. Bored to an end beyond all ends. Bones of contention are necessary for all of us. For people with obsessive complexes and for us also. One creates the other. Inconsequential, supposedly, just like the facts and figures of our lives. Here one day, down the Swanee River the next. Happy in our youth one minute, the next, out of our minds with stress and up to out necks in trouble the next. Whose line is it anyway? What's the number on my life? Who has the buttons and strings that pulls it all together? Wizards? Masons? Witches? That's just the local characters I'm on about, isn't it? Who cares about Palestine? Palestinians and jokers that's who. Who cares about you? You do, you and your guardian angels and maybe your family once and a while, but your not on their minds all the time, believe me. Live for the moment, but listen for the call for virtue and ethics.

Another year is nearly upon us, it's the day before New Years Eve! 2012. (Editing 2017) No end of nothing, just a lot of wind, literally. Conspiracy theorists will find what they are looking for and the rest of us will dodge the bullet (Metaphor) For those of you too stupid to know, a metaphor is an understatement in this example. So, who's for tea? Anyone? Great! Make mine herbal and a coffee after thanks, earthquakes? No? Great. How's business, ticking over? Great. How are the kids? Well, you know, same ol same ol, different Millennium.

Tempest battling on outside as usual, well, its winter with an attitude, best to don the wetsuit and take it face on. I love to swim in the sea in winter with gloves on of course, especially in the rain, the harder the better, its like swimming in the shower. You feel at one with nature and winters goddess wraps her arms around you with a great big hug of love and tenderness. We are the people, we live and breath, without us there is no machine, remember that.

The fearless fool, the fear free joker, the imbecile gifted if only for a moment, with something he knows little of. Smokers cough, it's a metaphor for warning signs, its what the millennium is all about, repetitive mistakes. Keep making them and nothing will seem real, life itself will appear to be more like Limbo.

Remote viewing on a collective level can lead to mass mind control. Freemasons are now communicating with me on a one to one level, this is the new millennium, a time of freedom for all (50 percent) of us Human beings. Freedom on a massive world wide scale. Do what thou wilt and if it be wrong, thou wilt find out sooner or later is the motto of modern man. Here where we live now, Planet earth, there are mental energies that astound us, infuriate us, enrage us, turn men into women and women into men, then they end up working in the sex industry and kill themselves.

Weather they like it or not. So where does that leave the rest of us, when half the population is struggling to control the other half, how? Prostitution, in the cafes or on the street, in the marriage safe haven or on the street. In the minds of our youth or on the street. Wherever yea may roam, you will find it, selling out for a million or selling out for a penny. Some people came cheap. What excites me is the challenge, to be faced with death directly and figure out its place in our society. Mother Nature doesn't appear to have a conscience, she indiscriminately destroys as much as she creates, or is it her opposite Lilith. Her astral spirit lives within the masses also, war is an act of collective will, it's a wave of genocide and rape of women and men, just ask anyone living with a sexually intrusive poltergeist.

Mental astral abuse, assault and destruction is also a war, or a bacterial disease on life, on humanity, the humanity of respectful well bred people of course, not posh, not poor, it's a simple fact that will be tested by both the rich and the resentful. Get me wrong if you like, but that's life. If you've been given a chance, take it, don't sleep with common people, stay away from them, they don't need your pity, they need your friendship, your help, so do privileged rich folk. Without the intersession of well balanced temperate mental interference all would be lost! Ah, how comforting is truth.

Both sides are at war with Mr. or Ms in between. Wont allow on one side unless you sell out, will destroy on the other because of spite. Rock and roll, politics, art world its all alike, run by the rich or you, if you sell your soul, strike a deal with the devil or already have unbeknownst to you and strike it lucky. The Devil knows who serves him or her and will help out special cases once and a while. Destined for fame and fortune yourself? It's a very small world we live in, very, very small. Chances are you'll figure that out. I have scratched the surface of fame myself, many, many times, and never quite got my foot in the door. Always wondering, "what the f...!" a lot. Making friends with famous or rich people, getting offers of leading roles in major west end productions, Record deals, then having the backers pulling out, television work on daytime T.V. nothing big time, just little stuff like playing didgeridoo for an Aborigine story teller, or Saturday night comedy sketches, or police crime catcher re-enactments e.t.c.

"Saw you on television last night, you where hilarious!" Yes indeed, but always on the B list. Worked with big-time directors up close as a musician or cameo appearance, no big credits. Bizarrely enough my picture seemed to always be hidden from public view. Truth is the powers that be wouldn't allow it, to hide it from the world for some unknown reason.

Advertisement for T.V. also, always ended up you couldn't really see my face completely. We are protected, mad isn't it? Then it starts to escalate, more jobs, still B list, more famous people meeting you at parties or backstage at some gig. Eventually you get used to it, stop questioning it and go along with the "I knew this was going to be a part of my life, but not like this. It can happen to anybody, and it does, many people who are destined for success met their favorite rock stars by destiny, one guy I know just as he was kicked out of acting school was stopped by a car on the street with some guy asking directions. It was the lead singer from his favorite bang Axel Rose! He couldn't believe it, "Signs" There will be signs. Never give up, your enemies haven't, those that haven't killed themselves because their garage band didn't sell any Records and it broke up after its first argument. Some people do this, first fall from the horse and boom! Dead. Suicide, over a cover band! So now

what am I doing, writing my 5th or 6th Book to you, whomever you are, in the hope of eventual success, it has to be! It's a very, very, very, small world! Keep going, one reason I was so driven during my years of exile from the music scene was because I had too many spelling mistakes to correct in my first book, bizarre, but true.

Sell, sell, sell! No more headers, this is my book God damn it. Ah yes, indeed, if you want published, get with the programme, sell, sell, sell! Schnell more like, Whoopah! Whatish! Whip them into shape, are you fired up! Negative energy following you around in millennium? Yes! More than before. Positive energy and spiritual forces also, more than before? Yes! I know why, its my job, its my job as a healer, as a spirit doctor, as a psychic medium.

It could be your job too, if you work at it, not if your just being good, that wont really help, and why? Drive. Driving forces that help you to continue to live freely, are forces that only professionals can achieve, because we leave them in the office after hours. Self defense with light is a normal part of our day, but it's a necessary part of out day, dealing with the public. Work and functioning locally are two very different things. The same forces are at play, it's a game to negative energies and spirits and gods and demons e.t.c. Be good and you'll only have to nurture their servants, other people. Be careful and you can help mostly everyone as you "Weave" your way through the streets doing normal things.

How's home life? Family becoming a little high maintenance? Christmas a little touchy? Hard work isn't it? Living. Some people are quick, during this time. Were still stuck in first gear this modern society of ours. Dragster society, before its started its finished. Everybody's dream these days is to be famous, except now its about education, not talent. Were all here together, for some of us its the realization that irreguardless to fame or money or success, your health and reputation are indeed your only real reward. Family and real friends, children and love, everything else is about money, to a degree. The rich man will always be with us in spirit, pushing us forward to succeed, selling the air we breath back to us. Conspiracies aside.

Conspiracies are all the rage at the moment, during a period of flux and reflux, people need something to believe in. I believe I have just had a major revelation. During a conversation with a person I believe to be a complete and utter fool, I realized he has very strong convictions. So strong in fact that I started to ask myself what he meant by check down inside me for my darkest part. As I asked myself what he meant by this, of course not actually thinking of what he meant, I suddenly became aware of my blood.

How it appears to move around the body, how I could feel where it was concentrating, moving here and there beneath my skin. Top of the head one second, around the head, down to my feet in one second. As I study this I am aware of why, its spirits, wherever they're at around me, my blood seems to follow, or perhaps some entity within my body. A sort of protector, or even an alien spirit that's following my own spirit-guides presence around my body. Hold your hands together and see if you can feel the warmth of the blood between them heat up. Take them apart and see how your mind changes, starts to rush more and think rapidly.

Breath in deep and try again to feel the connection of warmth in your hands, your mind stops wandering or racing, you breath more easily, no racing or strange thoughts dominating or controlling your heart beat. As a psychic I am aware of the constant movement of spirits, positive and negative, dark, bright and grey. Every breath we take keeps us safe from harm, keeps us relaxed, reassures us of safety or helps us escape danger. Revelations is now, 2000 to 2100, changes are part of human existence, Mother Earth spirits verses technological advances that are all born from her. Mother Universe wants us to create I am sure, she wants us to experiment but on her terms. We are here now to function as a whole, not as a destructive nihilistic assimilated slave race of technological freaksters. Why do we worry so about the state of the world because its our responsibility, if we are the mature ones, the respectable ones, who respect even the most idiotic fool you can find. The fool also serves. He is the victim, the victim that tries to rule the world, either his microcosm i.e. the street, or his macrocosm, The Earth. The closer we get to understanding ourselves, the closer we get to being better sheppard's for the rest. Human beings will always act as sheep, they will always follow, always be easily led, its human nature. Being a sheppard means taking on responsibility, not talking about it.

My alter ego is out, looking for less logic and more senselessness. Shouldn't we all be a little clever, mischievous and daring. The god of mischief is among us, aware not of good or evil, but of what appears to be logic and yet isn't. The logic of the joker, the spirit that rules over immature people or clever Trevor's. Wise men of the world of amateur comedians, the dark side of freedom, leering, bullying, jeering, name calling, curiosity as to ones sexuality, manipulation of innocence. We have among us a plague, unseen. Unseemly, immature longing for attention or excitement. Being "Bad", "Wicked" and dangerous, causing only small hurt and poking fun, to causing serious psychological abuse,(Even in the name of fun) but ending in serious results. While reading this, for e.g. what are you're hearing in your head, inner thoughts? Or voices? Its ok, we don't think your mad, we know your having little conversations in the privacy of your thoughts. Unawares, most of the time, but now, come to think of it, there is a voice on one side saying, "Think carefully" another voice interrupting with (?) Whatever, comes to mind…You will find fools are too busy in the moment to realize what the Joker is more aware of, i.e. "Thought" Have you ever spent a minute to listen to your thoughts? "I wonder?" "Why?" "Who?" "Where?" "Am I?" e.t.c. What thoughts we have, two sides to your brain, two voices, one person. Doppelganger? (Google it, or read my last book, A Mediums Dream)

You can claim some thoughts as your own, "I am!" "I will!" "Yes we can!" e.t.c. Its invigorating to see what's in the mind, isn't it? These days we not allowed in. We are told what to think, what to do, and where to do it. Have you ever taught yourself anything? Its all about thought. Be a fool, buy a musical instrument, teach yourself, then see if you need lessons. Lessons are the cause of destruction in many artists lives, killing the art. There is a school outside, not a school of idiots who learn by experience, but a school unseen, where you get all the support you never had before. Its not a place for jokers. Teach yourself to write, the world will suddenly appear to be filled with idiots that take more of an interest in you, even asking "Who are you" as they pass you on the street. Don't believe me? Give it a try. They picked up pens years ago, wrote a poem and were ridiculed by the ignorance of their peers, gave up and became amateur critics. Village idiot mentality exists in high society as it exists in the gutter. Write, sing, practice saxophone, paint, doodle, run, dance, then try and make a living at it. You may do well.

Indeed, indeed, now I have just moved out of Biarritz to Belfast, the place of my birth in 1969. Very important year for Belfast and myself. Found a flat four doors up from the Spiritualist Church on Malone Avenue by chance. The law of averages hold firm to universal forces sometimes. That's why the weather was so bad in the Basque Country, to force me out early, lost my deposit(Again) as always. Met some friendly people here in my birth town, although its freezing cold. Bracing the weather is good for your health.

So, my first experience with spiritualist healing in body went fairly well actually. Didn't feel entirely welcome, by some, and almost left because of the reception, but I stuck it out anyway just to see why I was being faced with obtuse stoicism. It turned out to be something more complicated and yet hard to explain, ill get to it later. Home sweet home. Been thinking of coming here for years, there are some friendly faces and some not so friendly like anywhere else. Ah yes, the next day, after a frightful night of mental battering by the local gobdaws fools, jokers, perverts and messers harassing me on the astral plane, I understand, why so serious. Plus its hard for some people to be inviting when faced with things as serious as astral harassment.

Yes folks, its serendipity all the time nowadays, or chaos and anarchy within our own macrocosms or personal headspace. Explaining the usually unexplainable, subconscious realms and eons of our psyche. Worlds within worlds, we keep going, we have to. Adults that maintain respectability constantly forcing their opinions of "Good behavior" on the rest of the Human Race. Squeaky clean wet bred well groomed nerds from nerd world with souls melted in self dysfunctional "Hell" passing judgment on the rest of us hairy Druidic city dwellers. I wear my hair long and I have a goatee now without mustache which is way too dodgy I think. normal magical beings know well the world of politics lies at the heart of every joker, every clown. You wont worry too much about them though, will you: they're only joking.

Druids are among us now, wizards, witches (Real ones) sorcerers e.t.c. still freemasons have always been the real "Secret society" they were the instigators of modern psychic divination for the white majority. Nature cannot be destroyed though, so neither can earth religions. Outside of our Hollywood interpretation of what theses entail or pertain towards. Spiritualist herbal healing energies of truly obvious power. Strong forces that are applied to our bodies that we know are real. If none of you can remember childhood experiences of spirit, you will love magical earth source energies as they soar through your body and prove that spiritual healing exists, as it changes you life and brings powerful people into it. After they finished burning to death all the herbalists of course.

Millennium, its Jacobs Ladder time my friends and an eclipse is on the way, a penumbral one I think. That means that our energy is being sapped by all the residual energies of Planet Earth. With meditation and concentration we will be 30% more made of light than normal. Everybody else will be under the impression that all will be well. They will leave the house wearing only T-Shirts and end up with a winter flu that will last all summer. Trivial problems are the virus that will eventually be our greatest adversaries.

Fame, it can visit your doorstep if you wish for it long enough. You could be stabbed to death on the street and have local fame in the obituaries, or be beaten half to death by the police for being Irish in the wrong place at the wrong time, spend 11 years in Jail, where you are beaten half to death by the screws or whomever. Fame itself can and will end up being your 15 minuets or your ticket out of karma. Destiny will decide.

Accidental Hero's

The Guildford 4, the Birmingham 6. Without false imprisonment they would never have played the role of scapegoat . Without scapegoats there would be no need for nuclear bombs today (Pun) These guys represent collective needs, to blame, the public needs to blame anyone but themselves. Kill or be killed, even those who blame in the wrong begin to represent the actual guilty parties. Like the A.N.C in Africa, if you're black you sympathize for freedom, its almost inevitable, not if your middle class it isn't.

So who gets shafted? The working class, that's who, not many middle class kids getting shot in the head on the London Underground for looking too Brazilian EH? Why police are ordered by their superiors, who in turn are ordered by politicians and presidents to beat near death, innocent working class people, to breed contempt and give the middle class a reason for segregation. Who gets shafted in our society?, Protestant and Catholic working class neighborhoods. Look at some of the areas working class people live in today, its to keep them angry, to keep them subjective towards the leaders, the Kings and Queens of modern society. Who is offering a solution, nobody but the tax payer. Booming Industry (No Pun intended) Blasted by insomnias cure, the heads of all are busted on their thrones.

Punishment without trial indeed, commonplace accident that some are well to do, with all the trappings of success and others are cast into an eternal void of large screen TV sets, The Star and the Sun newspapers scattered around, beer bellies up the yazoo, kids with pieced nipples, privates, unspoken places, tongues, lips, ears and elbows, segregation, is imposed by karma, not politicians. Cry freedom!

Not that I really care, after the life I've had, still some people hold onto their souls and have hearts, more so than many well to do kids that are brainwashed and spoiled, bullied by society to look and live a certain way. Middle class people have their own problems, karma, karma, cause and effect.

Cause and effect: What a header, you'll never live it down, you'll never survive the apocalypse, I've never seen anyone do it, why should you? Well "Honey Bunnies" you probably wont, most of you. Most of you will fail, fall, kill yourselves, quick or slow, be consumed by the astral orgy of astral predators and devoured, sold of as yesterdays news to a lower vibration spirit kingdom, jump from heights and tall buildings willingly or un-willingly, metaphor or non-metaphor.

Some of you will do it smiling all the way to the bottom, not just the metaphorical bottom either, the real deal either ends up in the end of all ends, or you suffer. Suffering is the opposite of stress release, who's selling the quick and easy way out? Jezebel, she's a low class shlapper, a drunken slag with a taste for superiority, delusional superiority, the kind the village idiot has, the kind butch or slim self-hating feminists have, loud mouthed abusers have, negative thought creators have (Men and Women).

Astral experimentation, that's all humanity is capable of, take the sugar and run. All the spirits of the firmament are around us now, coming through the molecular walls around us. Flying through the air, the waters, the ever increasing heat of the Sun.

People, people, people, you're possessed, were possessed a lot of the time, by demons, real ones, little ones, some of you even use the rhetorical expression as swiftly as foul and filth from the local skanger (Lost youths) population. These people are out on the street, hiding the real demons from the rest of us.

The rich people of The Earth (That's Planet Earth), coke addicts, alcoholics, charismatic celebrities, politicians, doctors, lawyers, dentists, judges, police e.t.c. Don't worry, they only visit us in our dreams. It's the poor mouth that visits us daily out on the street. It's the street that finds its way into our homes, through T.V. Media e.t.c. In Australia they are passing a law to ban flat-chested women from media advertisement to curb enthusiasm for perverts for under developed minds, the mainstay of Hollywood Movies. Hollywood invented abuse, it's a dangerous game perversion, you cant even breeze a quick look into Hollywood without obvious signs of extreme dodgy half naked "Wrong" screenplays plastered all over our lives. In fact the endorsement of philosophy for the everyman i.e. pansexual culture as a whole is now solidly embedded in our minds as normal endorsement. Take your t-shirt off it's a Hollywood movie not destined for adult eyes.

So, if you're wondering why you're suffering in life, its one of 10,000 things and more, you married a lazy sex addict, that's the fault of modern media advertisement, you've bred a bunch of teen boozers rapidly expanding the non-voting population of underage minors, duped into demonic spiritual activity by years of brain washing by the movie industry-media mainstream that sex is for self destructive downward spiraling rebellious creative types, and that's just the half/brain rated movies, where the star is hetero in character but the pansexual hedonistic orgy-mad coke sniffing mummies boy and destructively so in real life (Rock Hudson-not hetero, James Dean-don't make me laugh, Charlie Sheen-he is hetero). Subtly hidden behind sensual stereotypical role models who represent their realities in some of their on-screen alter egos in their spare time. God bless them, they're good people.

Whatever, its too subtle to bat an eyelid, that's just it, its so subtle its obvious. Colleges are filled with sensually erotic philosophical themes, subliminal and obvious brainwashing. Omega House, where you hang out with your frat buddies, statues of David outside in the park, ballet lessons for the wrestling team who are also forced to act hetero and overcompensate hedonistically yet also secretly trained to show major interests in omnisexuality, its all suggestion, nothing normal about it. The land of brainwashing has its foibles but nothing as bad as any other country, especially if you're from a society fracked with middle class demons born from jealousy and status envy. Come on, I'm joking! But seriously. When its all over your guilt will eat your heart out!

Our society has always had its hedonists, they always go to Hell, and they have a terrible time there, it sucks. Nobodies meant to go that far, but we humans, animals that we are, cannot resist. Its as if were brainwashed into it and there has to be an even number of failures who died having a really, really good time. God fearing Christians most of them. Hey, that's the power of suggestion buddy, sex, same sex relationships even today are absolutely sure that bisexuality is an evil that must be stamped out, sounds like they're projecting the worlds rejection of them. So the media tells us, constantly. Only socially acceptable sexual abnormality prone people make the headlines, no news is bad news. You nor me can offend socially accepted sexual abnormality. Famous people or ethnic minorities, repressed majorities and drug addicts for fear of being labeled bigoted or sued or attacked by the very same fascists of all sorts. Meanwhile some Hollywood screen writer is visualizing his next subliminally omnisexual movie that's sure to hit the future frat boys right in their homophobic football tighty whitey faces. Future black swans.

Boom, its offensive! Its bound to sell! Bisexuality is an evil in the eyes of gay people because it endorses equality for men, not feminists. That's bad for the other side, the opposite team, the enemy. Our hero, the man that endorses men, is surrounded on all sides by the tyranny of evil men and women, anything that opposes truth and goodness, fairness and loyalty. He's batting for the other side, means he's with the girls, he not one of us, means he is against us and pro-feminism-antilife (As opposed to feminism pro-life). So if he's sleeping with women and men, he is endorsing bisexual choice and male existence in a Universe that should be men free!. Some anti-men activists see all good men as evil, they represent a world of oppression, that's you and me, normal guys (Sinners)

The enemy, the bisexual or experimental male (Bi-curious) from birth he was bisexual, he has a bisexual brain, he's androgynous, respect his life choices, he's not fooling himself , monomaniacs are,(Pun). Bisexual people are harassed by both sides, gay people officially hate them, call them liars publically. Whew! Fascists! Keep out, stay out, be who you are, die happy! Its all a conundrum, but for a reason, imperfection attracts fascists that see fascism in you and me. We, the good people are beset upon from all sides by the evil and tyranny of ignorant clowns and jokers who make their own rules. They serve a purpose, karma, some fool has to. Balefully. Whew! Page over.

Alchemists

Due to unforeseen misrepresentation by the media, this next group is highly prized by the public domain as too open-minded. Missing the point of sexual experimentation by a hundred miles, the less fortunate of our in-educated population sees sex as a means to an end. Self realized people who have "Tried everything" (Legally and morally acceptable) find themselves ostracized by friends, family and subterfuge (Peers, judges, lawyers, school teachers and police...) because they are too experimental. They know this because of the bad press sent out constantly by notorious front page messiahs of rumored experimentation. The west has had 400 years of it throughout the industrial revolutions introduction of opium, brothels and politicos (need I remind you)

Who knows, maybe in 600 years we will again see a more open-minded society where people can experiment with anything and rest assured their recovery is guaranteed without so much as a blot on their golden reputation. Buda did it.

Experimentation itself theses days is a very dangerous thing, fraught with instant karma, or effects to the more lay persons mental orientated version of you. Effects of action i.e. reaction, don't know what that is? In education as to the results of a lifetime spent living supposedly square existences, whilst judging the rest of the world as a patsy/scapegoat for the vengeance of God, or the Divil, or karma or the white trash scumbags(How dare I!) (You know what it means, or do you) I spend most of my time trying to be supportive, its my job.

Go out in your 20s, have fun, shop around, beware the residue of the elderly, its everywhere, waiting in the shadows for youth, ready and waiting to pursue a life long dream of failure. It may well be recognized that many supposed idiots are just hiding their potential from the cool people, the siblings of their own families, the nemesi waiting in the closet. The true of heart know well the ugliness inside, they remember it from their past lives.

We all hold memories in our subconscious. Ever wondered why older people never liked you, why they seemed to hate and despise sensitive people of their own age? Self hatred, self disgust, they are victims of self oppression, "Could have been anyone, so could everyone" mentality. Too fat, too thin, too stupid, ugly, dumb, greedy, perverted, vain, sulky, cow-like, boar-like, beasts of the field. God bless the child!

Ah yes, the first warm days in May have finally arrived! Miracles are happening right in front of your eyes! Happy good natured good looking sensitive people are walking about the place, bizarre! Where in Gods name have they been hiding! Seriously, how come in the cold of winter there's a major shortage of beautiful wholesome lookers out there? It's The Twilight Zone meets Tales From The Unexpected. Still if there is a reason it must be a good one. Gods master plan to force us to see past beauty, to look inside and feel the presence of beauty within. Generally, I don't want to live in a world where fat is the new thin, even though cat walk girls are the new charity celebrities and some of them are known to eat full fat cheese. Believe it or not, there are people hiding all year round that come out in the balmy months of summer. Its like going back in time, to a warmer place, of joyous childhood where your selective memory rules and anything is possible. Gods of summer, I will follow you until the taste of Autumn calls again, I'm off to Cairo!

Fires of Passion

What burns within the minds of men, that gives us need and lust for fortunes greater than the shamed. What sacrifices will you make, to create some great new thing, some masterpiece, some New Age revolution, some new revelation that puts all before it to shame. Who will fall at your heels, who will die by the law, whatever that may be. What is ruling the hearts and minds of people with vision, clear headed patrons of the art of life, what stands in your way, fame? Fortune? Sex, Drugs and fundamentalist religion? Wash it all away, leave your life, your work, your friends, your dreams all broken and destroyed and walk the Road less travelled. Seek the mountain top, seek to speak your own truth, your own message. Rebel! Reveal! Conquer!

Were all imbeciles sometimes, I use this word to incite an eventual reaction in people. When you start to use it to represent people in general you find it starts to expand and cover the general population. The general population includes people who allow you to feel a connection with. Its addictive to us al, we all call people rude words, or curse foully at them or about them, or take our time ridiculing them throughout the passage of our lives. For me now the word imbecile is an anachronism, or a word that now describes idiots it's a word I follow mentally with "forgive me Lord" for my incredulity, allow me to make amends for my insults, help me avoid a reaction from these people when they subconsciously "Allow" tit for tat as collective conscious conspires. So its not a simple as it seems, we spend our lives affecting people without direct communication.

It's a compliment to compromise in a world gone mad from compromise. People compromise their dreams every day, in fact it's the reason for all suffering, compromisation of ideals. It all starts with dreaming and creativity, when you begin to create as a child whilst drawing pictures ,you are usually complimented. It's a miraculous experience for your parents, its wonderful to see the energy of love and light on paper, its all good and we should nourish it, it's a privilege! As long as your parents are sober and non abusive.

Normal childhood is a privilege we all should deserve, drawing on positive constructive parenting is natural and from my experience, normal. Thus the school of life is more important then education, to a point, as long as the School outside is one protected by enlightened people. It's the meaning of life, to exceed in all things, to understand the suffering of others after we are schooled by our parents. Suffering is usually ignored until it becomes an issue, but what of education before the fact. What of modern progressive education, does it exist? Where does it exist? In private education mostly.

Royalty, why it exists, natural selection, fittest and most well bred survive. Good breeding mostly is the reason why royalty expands from one place to another. When one country is colonized or massacred genocidically by another, it was usually the royals who fled first. They had the money to do so. Pride of place in the lesser scheme of things, special people with special energies to help them, manly because that's the way of nature. Nature represents people in all their foibles, and also endorses the powerful display of beauty. Beauty encapsulates, it can also make the greatest noise. It gets to rule the less beautiful, less privileged less good looking tax payers. Imagine how it feels to be a king or queen, you don't have to pay tax, back in the past.

Demi-God complexes here we come, you're even blessed by the magicians or Druids and have a spirit likened to gods, named after gods and blessed by them. Somebody has to represent natures need to dominate and rule, diplomatically.

Celts all had Kings, Barbarians, Bavarians, Pagans, War lords, covered in Gold and Silver, head to Toe in expensive clothes, even when they lived in Straw huts. Straw Huts built extremely well mind you, with Oak beams 40 foot tall. The modern view of Chieftains isn't the real picture, its how very well off Shamans would live, with herbal remedies to put our modern equivalent to shame, not even the harshest winter could penetrate their immune systems or their Homes. Religion? The best, Druidry, solstice, Newgrange, Stonehenge, Europe was at their mercy, and Mother nature under their control, as much as She would allow. Booming music, Art, Magick that could move mountains to come to their Prophets and rivers of gold, surely their royals were immersed in Glory and had the powers of their Gods at their fingertips. They could not but Love any obey the will of art, of music, of earth Religion, could not but want to allow all men to be treated equally to their place and live free. Free to think.

Who would want to destroy such natural balance with Earths sensitivity, who would not understand that in the next life you to could play in the fields of the lord as Golden beings living a life less ordinary. It was a crime that this culture was destroyed to make room for the invention of Anti-nature i.e. Industry for the destruction of equilibrium. Change must come through Demons, so all rich men were possessed by Demons. All colonized countries that become the thing they despise the most are possessed by the same demonic need to take, destroy and annihilate all hope of natural selection. History teaches us that the dark ages were a time of Philistines conquering Celtic countries to the destruction of their Art, religions and Royal structures. Impregnating more than their beliefs into their new found slaves for the love of Gold.

Perhaps the Modern industrialized World was always meant to be, perhaps not. They say that Christ is the Sun, the light, so who was Lugh then, Lucifer, the Angel or God of light? An understudy or the same God under a different name?

Was Christ just an invented name to cover up the truth? That modernity was an invention of alchemistry gone wrong? Earth religion got in their way, so they invented a new religion created form an amalgamation of all other religions come before it, without even bothering to full disguise the fact.

Fact is we will find out one day. Modernity was a choice, but who made it, who wanted all they could see before them, where did its origin or origins begin? Collective consciousness, who knows. Perhaps we were never meant to use anything but stone and Wood after all. Leave Gold in the Earth unless its eaten for healing purposes. Leaving us to concentrate on the mind alone. Look at Hindus, they used the mind more than anyone and worship still today the 7 Planets or more and have temples dedicated to each of them, huge, gigantic temples still in use today. Even the public that worship there pay good money in alms, for they believe its more than a placebo, are not skeptics, experience serotonin highs along with the spiritual vibration that comes with them.

Do you honestly believe that Jesus wanted to destroy the druids by killing them all and banishing all their snakes, you're an imbecile if you do. In fact it was imbecilic to orchestrate such an institution when there was already one in place that would have fallen to the temptation of gold eventually, so why the hurry? The druids tried to kill all Christians initially in Rome via lion, i.e. lions tearing yer head off e.t.c Interesting the lion represents druids even today, perhaps it's a metaphor for debate.

Debating the right of Christianity to try to better what God decreed to be the universal religion in the first place, first place, first in line, the Druids people. Millions and millions of us used to worship Tyrannis, Lugh, Thor, Brigit, Sophia, Diana, Dagda. We had churches, groves, layline planted megalithic structures all around the whole planet. Druids were the masters of the spirit and healing, stood beside all kings and queens for thousands of years. There was no threat to mother nature through un-natural industries and technology.

We are the lords of earth and we will eat all who contend us, fair enough? Perfectly fair, normal and possibly apt that the king of the jungle didn't want Christianity supporting a new world order that was the foundation of industrialized killing of the lions population of the world overspreading a conformity that in itself was the invention of modern Rome. Was Lucifer really behind Christianity after all, angered that his name was swapped for another? Punishing mankind with instant effect as mankind rejected nature and embraced the pollution of earth through their "New Religion" Synthetic produce. The wheel. After all, the Vatican is built right on top of Pagan temples.

Metalwork, electricity, oil engines, all new world, all 1000,s of years old in the heads of philosophers within reason, yet to be created but designed by the Phoenicians or Egyptians already.

Ahh yes, it's a small world after all. The Humans ate the lions heart, and gone was mother natures hold on our planet, for a time anyway. Before you knew it revelations were inevitable, the atom became the centre of attention when evil finally took hold and the reason behind industrialization finally manifested, the destruction of Mankind. Give a dog a bone, he will eat its marrow, give a man a bone, he will use it to kill another man, sleep and impregnate his wife, kill his children and rule in his place. Give a man freedom of will, he will rule all other men, eventually. One world order. It could be the end of all evil when there is no real opposition to any world country. One planet, one country, lets call it "Utopia" It will be reality when it happens.

By that time druids will again be allowed to form their own state and start again as the main religion of that state, to worship legally and practice freely all of Lughs and Dagdas rules and regulations. The circle will come round perfectly, not just as a pastime pseudo-reflection of its origin but as much or more as it ever was the legal worship of one race or people. That's what is was like for Christianity initially, a "new age craze" something the everyman could pursue, after he had failed to pursue any other religion properly before that, who wouldn't be impressed by the first touch of the light?

I have seen Lugh, seen Thor, seen Amun and Jehovah. I know they all exist as separate entities in their own right and can all be worshipped as one or mentioned in ritual or prayer. All goddesses as well Hecate, Isis, The Virgin Mary, all interconnected, all open to individual ritual or prayer. If your planning to tell your local priest you're a druid or a witch, you'd better be prepared to go above heads and contact the Pope for ex-communication from the religion you have been signed into as a child. Until you do, you're still signed into it. If you're parents didn't bother, you may one day want to become Christian, or Druidic or Buddhist or whatever, when you do, rules apply, one way or the other. Rules are good, they help define us, otherwise all we are is pseudo-experimental, open-minded.

Royalty, returned to powerful positions only under the new age religion of Christianity. Daughters and sons ready willing and ale to follow their fathers agenda of power for gold and Christ. Whatever happened in between was mostly up to Constantine, (Pun) generating God knows what in the meantime, ah yes, the decline of the roman empire (Druids revenge) Karma? Cause and effect? The vengeance of Pagan gods on Rome, the traitors city, built on Paganism, kept afloat on Christian donations and war-lords conquests. Richard the "Lion heart" for example, wasn't he a Templar off killing Arabs for Christianities name in Jerusalem. Kapow! One more co-incidence regarding names and what they represent. Its so obvious now we don't see it. The Lion also adopted by Christians as a Saint, St Mark.

I believe in Christ, I prey to Jesus every day. I worship his photograph and absorb his energy as Bruno Groenning, or Braco, the returned Christ (Google it)

He is Lugh, he is any Pagan god of the Sun, he is love, light and the God made man. I worship Shri Matagi, the returned Virgin Mary, she is the Mother of God, she has returned also, I have her Photograph also.

All who know these beings agree with me, fact. Tried and tested, wise beyond reproach, experienced and long suffering the frailties and failures of mankind and Womankind, god bless em. Man does not make history, we do. (Double negative? Oxymoron?) we are the ancient Pagans, Christians, e.t.c. ancient prophets, royalty, chieftains, druids, bishops, popes, celebrities, in this life, our past lives and in the next. We all want to be famous in this life because we are made to feel inadequate or inferior by our so-called ex slave masters who themselves hold the direct bloodlines to their ex-countries, the countries that populated the place they now live in as aborigines if only by DNA.

The rich today still hold their place by natural selection, by choice, accent, appearance, birthright, its OK to be a black man if you're a TV presenter if you have a posh accent, or can pull one off. You know whom you serve. Blonde Scandinavian really is beautiful, on the outside anyway! Yes?

CHAPTER SIX

At this stage of the game I have been manly practicing Planetary Magick for around 3 years (7; editing 4 years later). The first few initial stages bring empowerment and excitement. Initial stages that last 3 days, maybe more, that's it, just a taste of what could be, a little pep from the energies invoked or involved. After embracing magick completely as a Man and starting on a voyage of discovery from booklets about how to make your own white magick talismans to protect you from idiots and negative energy to more hard core defensive magick that, although it works, leads to the fire straight from the frying pan.

Why? Bigger energies invoked to remove jinxes of collective conscious karma can make incredibly big immovable objects placed there by the institutions of mind control very volatile. The Church, the Police, law and order.

Law and order also ignore the fact that chaos rules them continuously. This chaos manifests eventually in alternate ways. Its such a large topic, you could write a book on it. Plus its not something you can readily explain to innocent clients. The control of chaos is one golden rule of magick. The organic ever evolving ever changing energies around us serve to keep a sense of the mystic without the use of marijuana or alcohol. The study of magick is not one for self education or entertainment, its one of responsibility and a continuous need to serve good people. People who's problems are mostly from the bullying of more earthy physically or mentally obstructive "Cries for help" The removal of these problems are all in the mind. Magick can and will eventually create a harnessing effect on thought itself. Our thoughts are living spirit, floating through the atmosphere, both positive and negative. We choose to harness both sides interveniously throughout the day, as suits our needs.

Too much of a bad thing is disastrous, negative traits abound and negative people are hard to work, live or deal with. Positive people are well aware of this fact, they are unashamedly aware that real good vibes, energy, feeling, deeds and attitude is natural to them. So the battle rages on and we wonder why we have to suffer so, Magick is work, in magical terms, Opera. Opera is Latin for work, the work of the body in an opera singer is a world in itself, the strength of an opera singers diaphragm will be far greater than average peoples diaphragm strength. Volume isn't important, its tone, you understand tone, you're a mature young person aren't you? Ever babbling immature young men are a viral infection on the astral mental plane. Control looks easy, but the average fool has little or none, its all noise for them, all chaos and anarchy and confusion.

All ancient cultures were about tone, tone is control, the control of subtle energies, the energies of life, people, emotions, nature and the spirit-world. Who can control theses things? Musicians know all about tone, good musicians that is, bad musicians know nothing of tone and kill the art.

Magicians subtle art is perfected style, druids, sorcerers, how subtle yet powerful their words of power, supported by knowledge of hidden secretive things known only to a select few. These secrets are powerful only to those strong enough or sensitive enough to see their energy after long intensive studies of Human behavior, animal, vegetable, and organic matter, stellar cosmic energies and movement. Its open to us all now, just as collective consciousness is also since the first day of the Millennium.

A friend of mine asked me why animals connect to Humans, weather its calling someone a "Dog" or worshipping a dog headed god. Why do negative entities manifest as animals, why wouldn't they, living physical creatures vibrate stronger than any other manifestation. On this earth everything manifests via some animal or other. Bugs/Aliens/Humans, metaphysically morphing into representations of spirit and mental molecular situations.

Its all written on the wall, look and you will se, seek and yea will find, the truth of everything. Other Worlds that exist all in the mind. You know much already but are you ready for the vibration of the truths that you have found. Seeing dogs with the souls of men or men with the soul of dogs, acting like dogs and women too, also acting as dogs.

Just today after talking to a young person, beautiful, forceful, strong, confident and proud, multi talented struggling with obstacles that equal their karma perfectly. That's their personal politics, the karma blocks that make up their lives, sibling rivalry they're not yet fully consciously aware of. Jealousy, politics, and personal politics, what clothes they like, music, people, types of people, hair, personalities, choices, it insults some people that they are not involved with the choices other people make regarding their company.

So the dog in us comes out, defensive, loyal to all we think respect us, even when it sometimes doesn't, doesn't treat loyal friends well that is. Embarrassed of nothing, not what happens on the weekend, the kind of things that animals do regularly, humans think certain things are acceptable yet are still subjected to ridicule by less open-minded, "Square" judgmental people. Being judged by moral high-ground personalities affects the dog-like personalities, makes them act more like animals and there you have it, cause and effect.

Also in European countries the dog was eaten for 1,000s of years, eaten worldly actually. Its place in our animus is fixed for eternity and that's a fact. Our eternity.

So, if you're opting out of sex, you will find those who are not will ostracize you, you're not running with the pack, you're contending with their place and rank in peer society. You are the lone wolf, the messenger, the vagabond, the scape-goat, the middle child, the recluse, the celibate, the hermit-spiritual outcast and you'd better get used to it. There's nowhere to hide, you will be sniffed out, both by the squares on your left who seek to find only the vibration of your animus yearning for love and physical comfort and the jokers to the right, who disown you because you reject their world, the world of accepted modern normality needs realized, sex, alcohol, physical comforts and al their hangovers and baggage.

The in-betweeners will react to peer pressure and rejection or fight back with healthy options, not smoking, drinking or sex. Big choice the last one for many, sex is the biggest drug, the strongest pull, the greatest fear, impossible to give up, ignore, forget about. It's the doggiest of Gods, the last frontier, undisclosed to all cultures its effects on our lives, our futures, our pockets.

Most people cannot listen to spiritual explanations about sex, don't want to, aren't ready to, afraid to open their minds to certain truths. Our western culture is still un-developed, un cultured and cluttered with conflict about the subject. That's for another book entirely. Yet the animal inside of us needs to feel free enough to think its human, normal and accepted by its peers. We are all afraid sometimes of being rejected, that's why as a spiritualist its important to socialize, even if only astrally.

Who invented astral travel initially, cave dwellers? Beings from a quiet dimension where spirit rules over the loud, crude forefathers of idiocy and animal instinct. Fair leads to foul some might say, pompous idiots, eh? Nimrods for the inter-personal anti-Christ, anti-Life, anti-Goddess Nebula, eh? Its good to laugh, isn't it!

The study of silence is a wonderful and beautiful thing, although many anal beings will disagree. Apart from playing music or practicing trumpet, driving your neighbors crazy for an hour a day, your quiet hours are part of your life experience, turn the music low, listen to the rustle of the wind in the trees outside. Let the cool Summer air circulate and remember, always, always be vigilant. Its part of Buddhist teachings that vigilance is necessary, its not space out and let yourself go time, its meditate but with energy, be energized in silence, ready for action, ready for high vibration astral projection, astral travel, its important to be completely awake when awakening to spiritual presence, rising up the ladder of metaphor into an alternate consciousness. Not many people are fully aware, nor have the time or privilege to be.

Ordinary problems or necessary needs, like wanting rich food are to be kept at a distance whilst living spiritually. Bigger and bigger problems are a sign, something is wrong, time to run, or emigrate, or prepare for wisdom and enlightenment to find a solution. The best lessons are learned by experiencing something in motion, in place, in the moment, via spiritual guidance, a helping hand, not a crutch. The Dali Lama would have been coached slowly, a day at a time with sensitive subtle energies unfolding like the petals of a flower. A druids cure, the petals of a rose, or hawthorn flower, who knows? We do.

Flowing waters, rivulets and streams reveal shapes that repeat themselves in our minds eye after watching them dazzling us into the Sunlight's reflection. Nature Spirits move the branches of trees to tell us things or show us patterns or shapes,, air spirits, angels connected to the elements, making them elementals. Wisdom is absorbed and passed on through communication, its something we adopt through careful meditated techniques, no need for pen and paper really, though we still need doctrine for study.

Astral Experimentation for All

Astral projection, or travel, for those of you in the know is happening subconsciously, you're doing it all the time. For the places and people that are available to you astrally now in Astral reality millennium is light-years ahead of dreary old pre-collective molecular astral existence. We are in a new world in 2013, a journey of discovery for all. Each of us experiencing revelations daily, nightly. New feelings born of suffering that will lift us higher and higher with less yo-yoing into the lower plains of karma and fear.

That's if you make some luck for yourself, quickly, avoid doing things that are pulling you down and be careful of what you're doing both mentally and physically. Coming from the modern world, as a student of life you have your Laptop to keep you company, your astral ascension can expand into places hitherto unknown physically just by watching the screen. To and fro, energies intertwining, huge energies bringing up the blood as astral flight returns to your heart again. One day at a time, one person at a time, the story continues.

Whereas I and you are in a new World Order already, because of spiritual situations imposed on us every 1000 years or so, or every time The Universe is changing into another level of consciousness. Our consciousness is undergoing a huge change. Collective consciousness has arrived! Its void time, soon will be void verses Paradise, I'm still writing, still working, still keeping my celibacy, as far as being with other people goes. Still reveling at the amazing revelations that have eventually arrived at your doorstep. You the reader, the public at large, half of them anyway, you the dreamer, the scapegoat no more, we can hope. Hope is the secret now, dreaming the dream of reality again, 2013 is as different as it can be for all of us, it really is a time to be as good as you can be. The year to open the divide between happy with what we have and those who will never be satisfied.

Revolution is in the mind, the best kind or rebellion is evolution. We have experienced a shift in consciousness within ourselves that awakens our inner voice, our personal space is sacred now, we all need to reflect on our lives and become excited about the possibility of life itself. A functional life.

Your spirit-guides are always communicating with you, have always been and may always be. The other non-friendly critic troll-guides are always about also. Its best to ignore them as much as possible, salting your home will help a lot, sprinkling salted water on the floor of every room. Open your windows more and let the cool breeze enter, get some fresh air in your Lungs, embrace life more and lift yourself up above the mundane plain of sex and love addiction and negative thoughts, stop holding your breath and face the day with the choices presented to you. What God does your people worship? The good people, the families and the pillars of modern society. Who holds the power of this God? Angels do.

Now, not to forget the devil in your day, just after I wrote the last paragraph yesterday a stressed out neurotic woman called me. She was very fast, quick, too quick for me. I told her I saw a child, perhaps a boy in the first card, she told me her partner and her decided to have an abortion recently and the child would have been better off not being born because of their financial situation. Then she asked me what I thought, was it a good idea?, here was my mistake, I should have told her I wasn't allowed to talk about health issues, but she was insistent and again very fast to ask me for my opinion, so I said, "its never a good time to do that". Not really a comment on health, of course, but then she back tracked and said she was going to report me. Bang!, after 6 months of beating them back I get sidelined. Oh no, I never did nothing bad in my life, says the imp.

I couldn't believe it, what did I say wrong, my job, my only real source of livelihood in a world of rip off companies taking advantage of the worker. I was very put out and angry at this attack, even sorry for the soul of the recently aborted child. I'm not stupid, nor do I voice any opinions about pro life but after this today, I'm a bit annoyed at the energy behind this persons assault on my ability to exist also.

I'm still waiting for the reader bashing call from the people I work freelance for. I am my own employer, I work for myself, I take calls and I read sometimes for face to face readings, but just rarely. People are dangerous now more than ever and the reasons why are always about the spirits behind them. Millennium spirits of change, opposition, chaos and anarchy. Angels of course, are never needed more than now.

Transference of anger is a big problem, from one person to another, its like a plague. I became angry afterwards, very angry, had to take half a Xanax for the first time in 6 months. Feeling blocked in and cornered now waiting to see if the company calls me, hoping I still have a job tomorrow. If not, well we will see eh?

So far so good, well see later. Hate is a powerful energy, it guides some people towards the gates of some un-discovered country, through a doorway of new possibilities where they gain the power to change our lives. Hate is possibly the earliest true awareness of individual thought, of personal tastes and of choices that help some people live as they please. Hatred of one race over another, of one sex over another, of religion, culture, class, music, fashion e.t.c. even drug cultures have their hate cliques. It's a normal part of life for us all, we all experience it and we are all forced to suffer because of the things we hate. We all avoid living in squalor because we would hate it if we didn't, but some people do not avoid it, therefore we are unaware that they think we are judging them by being clean. I didn't know the fascists were going to annihilate my whole race, I wasn't watching my back! I was lost in a world of butterflies and angels good luck with that, says the Divil.

Humanity verses inhumanity. All throughout history civilized countries have acted like dirty animals towards the people they hate. Colonization spreads good genes through forced pregnancy and murder (Romanic Britons law of Primae Noctis), therefore hate is necessary. Slavery too a necessary evil that spreads good genes into white communities and creates amazing new hybrids of us all. Bad things bring good changes, just look at extreme feminism for example. It takes a demon to overcome the demons of the past. Change must come through the barrel of a gun. Industrialization is evil towards nature, but given time will eventually save the planet from natural destructive forces, Sun Storms, meteorites, Communists with nuclear bombs and drunken trigger fingers. We are here for a purpose, existence is only a building block for spiritual awareness. Its great to hate you might say, oh but its not, its Hell.

Heaven on the other hand is great, but oh so hard to attain when your attacked by hellish demonic forces on a daily basis, subtly of course, no conspiracy theories here. We are always overcoming negative things, T.B. Aids, Cancer, Child trafficking, drugs, imps at night or day e.t.c. Were doing very, very well, remember, you're part of a group of people who are responsible for what they say or do, you will always be under the gun of ignorant idiots and immature imbeciles ranting and raving about how they are the victims and we all must pay, that's what jokers are, victimizers.

Be powerful, be strong, be ready, and prove your better than your enemies, be richer in spirit than them. Sell to them their salvation and watch them follow suit, eventually, then watch them try to sell failure back to you, Lucifer complex.

Now, Millennium-Supermoon madness is all about connections, past life soulmate connections, collective consciousness throughout the whole planet for all. Higher level consciousness for those who can rise above all of this, Children have a head start, so too do elderly people, disciplined spiritual people, nature and animals.

People call me, or call into my home-office everyday looking for explanations as to the person they have just met and how amazing the connection with them was. Leading most adults to think they have at last met their life partner after decades of searching. Then 2 weeks after sleeping with them are confused as to why he wont call them or is losing interest. I tell them, its all about this crossover period for humanity.

Our spirits are being awoken to higher order consciousness, blissful experiences await us if we are good, disciplined and wise. Its wisdom that's the key, think about how after 13 years of this new millennium we have arrived at a doorway to a new understanding of where our Planet is at. With this new awakening we have activity inside of us, mentally and spiritually. Most of us are experiencing connections we have never had before, never dreamed of. But, as a working psychic-healer I study the situation carefully, in detail. I have found that when I too make a new connection that I remember to ask God, or my spirit guides to show me the way.

They say follow the potential, raise the energy, go with the flow, allow yourself to be carried along with the amazing energy, then absorb it. As if this new person is sent from the stars themselves, we can almost touch their core and revel in the poetry that is their true selves.

Then, for some of us, we move on, to tomorrow, where another amazing connection is waiting in the wings, another past-life soul-mate arrives on our doorstep and it starts all over again. Something has found its way into our lives for the sole purpose of awakening our spirits feelings or need for flight. Where there's a way, there's a reason. Hug yourself, send it to them and release with a kiss on the back of your hand, its done, eternal attraction connections.

The reason? Well for me today as is the conviction of a sound experienced mind, the woman of my dreams did arrive again, of a Thursday. A God given angel with all the past life glory Astral transference can bring, again she is connecting with me afterwards all day, with all the astral frills of love and joy, its amazing!

Who needs to go any further? My clients i.e. you people. Can you see the light? Or fall into temptation without a magick ring on your finger? I know how to deny temptation, first give in to it, then develop it. Meditate on the next person you have an "Amazing" connection with, tune into their family, their angels, their nieces and nephews, see if you also, like me can enjoy the "Real" reason we are having past life connections in this miracle of times.

Today was tough for many to get through but because I rose above it I will attract winners, customers who call to my door looking for advice or ancestral connections from the spirit world, both living and in spirit. The higher order of spiritual energy, God, good karma, luck, call it what you will, is serving us when we pass these temptation-attraction tests. Cosmic tests and we've had nearly enough years of them now. Portals upon portals, that's what we are. Acting as either vacuums or stars, black holes or white pulsars. Energized or vampiric, its up to you to decide.

So anyhoo, onwards and upwards, before you know it, you'll be wondering who or what will be next, what temporary place they will have in your life. What message they bring as you bend backwards to tune into their wave length and bring some light into their lives. The Universe was always watching, its you who were blind all along. Ever tried living as a monk or nun, hermit-Buddhist, new age spiritual being? It's a great amount of work, that is if you have the work, if you're a working bedsit shaman tuning into The Universe and living in a Limbo-like existence, its all temporary. Wait till your friends see how great you will become! Your spirit rising far above your id. Free from ego, free from material sufferings.

Have you found your way out? Tarot, crystal ball, medium? Singer, dancer, Juggler in your spare time, herbalist, struggling Reiki healer, masseuse. Whatever your escape plan, and its worked, keep going, work is good, staring into the TV. and connecting to aliens is good too, but only for a short while. Everything we do now is about the great work, the work of working professional healers. Shamanic Limbo on the dole semi-professional decades of "learning" is over, dead, Finished. Welcome to mundane miracles.

Challenges beyond the norm can only be met with balanced experienced professional healing energy. Lourdes or Reiki, take your pick, like me, id go for both. Having positive, experienced people to connect to, whenever you need them is vital, they don't mind you calling for their presence. But don't forget positive spiritual energy from people comes with a connection to them, we have to be careful we don't attach our fears or our problems to them.

This is a big part of the politics of spirituality, we all have klippoth attached to us (Google Klippoth) spirits of negative energy. As we call for positive people to send us some light we open the Doors of the Mind. So, being aware of helpful peoples well being means guarding against dangers that might befall them.

Many Reiki healers find that they start to develop their clients illnesses if they forget to earth themselves whilst working. So if we call for people to connect with us, they are opening up to the reasons why we called for their presence in the first place.

Its like passing into the light whilst attaching to another person, not a good idea. We can all pass into the spirit world even when were still alive and work together to find a blissful clean energized state. Purity of body is vital for both sexes. There may be times when this is possible when chatting to people throughout the day on the astral mental plane, astral telepathy. Trust is a huge part of it.

The foundation for successful telepathic astral support or communication is purity. A clean body makes for a clean and confident mind.

CHAPTER SEVEN

We are made up of different parts, under the influence of spirits that have been a part of out psyche since we were put here artificially(At least that's how it appears) by forces unknown. The race to overcome all obstacles is one of the many meanings of life, the greatest obstacle being many manifestations of divine logic. If we get our way were done for, success of one person insults the failure of another. Why one person becomes a success and another a failure is because of bad habits in thought. Thought alone lets us win or lose, live or die, be or begone. Self preservation is fine, but fear and greed must be the work of opposing forces creating energy, weather created by thought. In the

beginning there was thought, before word, before sound, before the 1,000,000th billionth time the Universe has gone bang probably. Thought was born out of nothing, doubtful? Hard to grasp?

So against all odds we exist. Scientists cant explain many phenomenon especially there own reason for being and where all life originated. Answer me this, why did the big bang have to happen? Why couldn't there have been nothing to there explode in the beginning and where did all that physical material come from in the first place?

Long ago, was there no gas, no dirt, no water, no nothing, no space? Then we here did it come from Noah's Space machine! Boom! Evolution is based on the idea that all life exists because the Universe expanded in the first place.

I know, it just happened, its impossible for there to be nothing, or is it? "MU" the Chinese call the Universe when it retracts back into itself and also enters an alternative state of nothingness. It's a lesson in how to keep interested in life, how not to become bored with the meaninglessness of a tawdry existence. Even with god you must suffer a certain amount to keep your sympathy with humanity or your congregation if you're a Buddhist Monk, suburban human e.t.c.

Its an enigma wrapped in a shroud of hope that all will be explained, if you keep it together. In fact I'm best at keeping mystery afloat, its all in the wrist, know? Think about it, Human beings have always had major challenges, major upheavals, trials and tribulations throughout history. The dinosaurs had it hard too, it's a fashion that follows being here. We will always have to work at it to get it right, even more so when we do to keep it right. That's what we in the First World have. Those of us who were privileged to have been born into comfortable homes and lives, even those who made do with less and made better lives for themselves without. We have to work at it to keep our lives together, it natures law. We are governed by nature still today. Until were sending stem cells into outer space in test-tube laboratories for the cultivation of empty planets.

Stuck in the mundane worries of this world? Not all of us, some of us shirk the "Norm" and embrace the impossible. The big time is for all, rich and poor, we can all contribute with hope and faith and charity. The greatest world leaders can be born from a very meager existence and vise versa, they can also come from rich families too. Get into the spirit of the thing, see that your life is worth living, worth waiting for the good times, the Summer months, the heat of a Winter fire, the joys of

Spring, the auburn leaves of Autumn.

Governed we are by the forces of others, battle them we must. Ghost-busters got it right when they realized spiritual activity affected the living, making all spectral entities curious to our existence. We think we have personality clashes throughout our day, when in fact if we open our minds and ask as to what's really going on we begin to see clearly.

Right now a woman of curious disposition is floating in the atmosphere of this day, out on the street beyond, I ask "What" in my mind and I am clearly shown a large green worm-like spirit sitting in front of me, I ask "What" again and am shown a snake-like movement of energy moving from the left of my apartment, through the streets and up towards the hills beyond. I now communicate with the spirit directly and it tells me clearly " I am weak" it shows me also the inside of its forearms, the telltale signs of heroin use, or some other drug. So as the why it chose this floating female to connect to me is becoming clear, she is affected by this very same spirit. Perhaps it has latched onto her somehow.

"L" is the last letter of her name I am told. Carol, Isabel, Abbeygale (phonetic L) I'm sure we will meet at some stage, but right now its all I can do to stop becoming this specters next victim. Incense, salt and discipline is the solution.

These things have their opposites also, and a busy man has no time for negative energy anyway. So, then, a choice enters our lives, get busy fixing things by listening to your higher angels and getting along nicely when mundane energies try to enter your lives.

Martial arts are a great way of concentrating the mind and giving you focus. If you're interested in Chi-Gung for example, you know after a while your able to both use it as a defense and also as a Spiritual awakening, the kind of person that has a natural way of exercise, like playing their guitar or bringing up children is also flexing muscles and building stamina. Smoking or non smoking its all good in moderation until you have to stop smoking for health reasons, or the music industry isn't for you, or parenthood leads to flabby bellies that need seeing to. Callanetics works miracles.

Mundane energy, boredom, apathy, sloth and ill health eventually leads to stress. We cant all be stressed just because somebody else is. We cant all be fat or thin, ugly or beautiful inside or out, differences are out natural state.

So, when customers call me and don't know how powerful they are, because they cant feel there own strength, I tell them (With light and spirit) I wheel and deal with or without cards, with or without inspirational angels of the Sidh, gods or snake spirits, crocodile spirits, butterfly spirits, spirit children or whatever wants to help them see. Help me, show me, how.

I try to get customers to see, that its time to rise up the ladder, to a higher plane, that's why their being tested so harshly by certain forces. Contending forces. The animus verses the ID. or the sex drive verses the higher order angelic nature within us.

The forces we contend with, all of us, are battling with each other, struggling for equality under their own rules.

Wow! Cant start a new chapter here but, I've just landed in Antibes in the south of France. Decided to leave Belfast after six months to dodge the yokels. Just a couple of mad weeks leading up to it. My Uncle Bernard died last week, or had his second birth as I call it. Spent the week at home to dodge relatives, I hate funerals.

Into the great unknown, for him and I'm off to another exciting adventure searching for new places and people. Getting here was hard, so much effort travelling by bus, plane, feet. Spiritual obstacles along the way trying to take my energy and weaken my will power. Hotels with uninvited guests, "Non Draco!" Jealousy and competitive spirits all the way.

Through the airport onto the bus in France, after carrying 25 kilos weight of bags along the streets finding a nice hotel "The Star" for fifty euros, then being woken at four in the mourning by drunk teenagers banging esoterically for hours and hours. Bang! Slam! Cough, laugh, grunt, waffle, Bang! Lift, drop lid, toilet flushing, more banging, coughing, moving furniture? Moving more furniture? To the left of me, right of me, below me, calling downstairs to get them to shut up, again, and again, and again. I could feel the flapping of large wings aiding their secretive disturbing energies that complimented this ballet of negativity. "Non Draco"! I call again whilst imagining decapitating them one by one in front of each other, just for the pleasure, "Jesus forgive me".

Maybe I shouldn't have come here, maybe the phone isn't a land line in my new Pad, maybe its an Internet Phone. Oh God, this is too much, I'm going to cry like a little Girl. No, I'm a Man, I can do this, I bet you this is all going to work out, and, it did. Here I am, all moved in the a pad put together by Angels, perfect little Flat beside the Sea, wooden floors, Children playing everywhere, Peaceful and tranquil, wow!

Kapow! Just 700 or odd years ago the templar Knights were disbanded, burnt at the stake e.t.c. I find as I google that date for last nights mysterious circus of horrors. In this day and age, something is also happening, through human consciousness and human ego. Perhaps they are the two dragons of old, ego verses ID. So, one day on and what a difference a day makes, looking for martial Art classes, Tai Chi, Judo, Kung fu, I wonder what will it be.

I'm contesting with the egos of ghosts and residual energies of those in spirit, also with the doppelganger mental telepathy of my neighbors. I love to think that I will be contesting with the will of my neighbors after they have passed into the spirit world. You see to know too much can be a plus sometimes. To know that good intensions are the cause of all sorrow. I intended to compensate for my failures with good intensions. Even the evil thoughts of people are laced with the purpose of intending to offload their foibles in exchange for ours.

Catch 22, the gates of Purgatory are upon us, the Gates of Paradise are above us, one is throwing out Toilet water, whilst the other is praying for freedom from the same. Oxymoron macrocosmic revelations, on with the games. On with empty promises, on with the prevention of war and the use of chemical weapons, its all metaphors. Why do idiots give so much to charity, because they have to. It's a temporary reprieve from karma, its fashionable. The power of glamour.

The Goddess of celibacy Kali is upon us here, arms being lopped off on the spirit plane, heads rolling on down the street, shopping for egg corns. New shoes! Knees cut off for an instant, people are getting used to it, especially around here. Still only a psychic seer can see directly, all that ails us. The Gods still answer us from long ago, because its still their planet, Christianity didn't banish anything or anyone, the spirits of Druids live among us, invisibly, perhaps Mother Nature has a plan for us after all, just like in the old movies when the forces of nature are at the beck and call of divinity. If there are Roman soldiers spirits seen by psychics and public alike, standing guard still 1800 years after placement in England, Scotland's boarders and Dublin Ireland, then the Druids are here in spirit, loud, proud and as powerful as Jehovah himself right!

Children are the cleanest spiritual energy around us, glowing with golden light! Old people too are free of all their inner karma, if they're lucky. So get busy being good or the Goddess will get you. Know when to stop being an idiot, know when your time has come, know how to start seeing angels, when you're listening to them, not asking them questions. We arrived here on a form of transport, but will we leave on it? Will you be happy knowing that purity and innocence are the keys to the spirit world, carry on as before without trying every possible way to hold onto something so many underprivileged people have never had.

Take action in a world gone a little mad, and seek only the sane, seek only like minded people and start rejecting those without true maturity. Writing this and knowing, or hoping that a meteorite or comet may be passing by, and that it holds no threat to me or mine. What of those who party hard until they can party no more, most of these people I used to know are now passed on by disastrous means.

So many of my customers have all the same situations in their lives, infidelity, fear of leaving redundant marriages, fear of rejecting ex partners as they return to get their laundry cleaned and their meals fixed. Fun, isn't it.

Saturday brings light, powerful full Moon penumbral light, I love this energy now that we are suddenly more aware of its effects on us. Penumbral is the new "Buzz" word for me, it's a hugely challenging experience and right now there are comets flashing by, Sun storms booming down on us, aurora borealis magnificence and penumbral eclipses causing us to invite un-natural amounts of light into our auras. I'm stunned to silence and last night walking over the cliffs here in Antibes the moonlight started to prove itself to me, slowly moving over the water through the clouds towards the shore. The presence of spirit was strong, brotherly spirits calling me to Spain. Starry skies on the way home and huge dark clouds towering high into the sky like pillars offering a pathway to paradise if goodness rules.

Today, the day after the eclipse the Sun feels feminine, and oh yes I forgot to mention, supposedly the Sun has flipped its poles this month. First major sign (If its true) that The Earth is getting ready to do the same.

My crystals are almost levitating with bulging
energy after I covered them in mandrake oil
and left them to the Moons rays, kapow!

Rewards for 14 years of suffering. Il Paradiso! Or the other place if fail (Not an option right?)

Wow, how quickly we change and move with the cycles of The Earth, how demanding people are these days! As each personality makes its daily demands on us, we have to sympathize with them or try to connect with their humanity. Living in cities teaches us eventually that the grim faces of the street-seller can crack into a wide smile and laugh as we decide to be jovial with them. Its their way of saying congratulations! Welcome back into the world, making do with what you have.

Make do with your attack on negative faces and find the human being within, if they soften to your wit, sometimes they do, sometimes not, that's their problem.

That's microcosmic politics, the politics of personalities. The philosophical mind of a professional healer is recognized by other healers and by some clients, who may become healers themselves. Productive people, alive and well in pre 2030, as the world turns and we are still here, and all is good, goodness rules.

So many celebrity lookalikes he's and she's connecting with me now, or is it the real deal? Or is it just always lookalikes? For many years I have seen celebrities visually connecting with me on the astral plane, sometimes its them, other times its their lookalikes. Literally living in alternative universes. The glamorous illusion of self delusion leads nowhere but down I'm afraid.

Universe upon universe, kablam! If fame has its own special kind of light, then perhaps all of us who believe that famous people are somehow connecting with us through their photographs e.t.c. are just availing of natural formats of connection. 1,000s if not 10s of 1,000s of people watching or thinking or dreaming about certain celebrities throughout the career of said famous person. That's a lot of energy, gods are born of such energies. "The Muse" for example, is fed by all creativity, breeding more productive creativity into our next generations dreams and ambitions. Or meteoric burn out. Shuffle.

Spirits born before Humanity existed, spirits of elementals and of their creators. Organic creations from nothing, from the energy of the big bang. Creative energies, living entities that had to be. After all something had to be created from Nuclear explosive forces so huge and incomprehensible. The one true enigma, what was before matter, before nothing, before …

We are the icing on the cake of life. We live on a planet born from other planets. Where did they get their gasses? Their waters, from the explosive heat of the Big Bang of course. Only Gods know.

The physical manifestation of gas represents divine energy. Formless energy able to move wherever it likes. Eventually giving life via amoeba from some kind of fungus. Human beings can be traced back to a fungus from millennia ago, our first ancestor was a fungus. Break an atom, you get a mushroom cloud, co-incidence?

Creation is another form of the creative process. It has always been a means to an end. Drawing animals on a cave wall to help manifest dinner, must have worked, therefore its purpose is to control our environment. We are a construction of thought, of something else's thought, God? Divine energy, Gas?

Gas giants rule our Seven Planet system, why? Gas is powerful, we breath it, it fuels our brains, oxygen of course, not cyanide(pun).

Gas is form, it is life in its earliest place. Elements and "Elementals" are created by it.

Fire Elementals =Salamanders

Water elementals =Undines

Earth Elementals=Gnomes

Air elementals=Sylphs

The searching for one thing will find another. Here's the rub of a lifetimes work, the sorting out of opposites, every Librans task. When customers call me, or call to my door, it's the first thing that comes to mind sometimes, are they sane? Are they on their life's path or are they rummaging through the fields? Seeking a world that pertains to what they think sanity is, doing everything wrong.

What element rules their day? Fire and earth? Are they all, "On Show" parading themselves as examples of humanity, then what of self defense? Fire and earth?

If during the millennium we find ourselves being checked by others, by the elementals ruling over them, at that moment in their lives, then we are subjected to the elementals. The spirits running the show, not God, not angels, but energy. It's the energy of chaotic natural forces, Wind, Fire, Earth, Air. Each having their own lesser and greater spirits.

God, may just be the collective energies of all four elements by their prospective elementals. As human beings were created, so too Gods began to appear, energy manifested as men and women, people started to "See" spirits via clairvoyance, psychic mediumship e.t.c.

Animals "See" spirits also, therefore too did some dinosaurs. But what spirits did they see, perhaps they saw us visiting them from the future. Nothing unnatural. We will time travel, it's a given. Astrally some of us already are.

Cavemen painted people with lions heads, because they saw the spirit of Leo, or the merging of lions with humans elemental energies.

And there Gods began to emerge. Elephant headed spirits, spirits without a head-Jehovah? Since millennium began I have begun to see peoples heads disappear. Their spirits changing? Or a message as to where we are. Weaknesses in their spirit? Hands disappearing or changing shape, through sight only of course. Had chicken for dinner? Noticed your skin suddenly looking like that of a chicken, just for a second, maybe longer? Even appearing to have tofu teeth? Imagination? Manifestation.

Manifestation of changes. Can we live like this, yes we can! Can positive thinking help us, yes it can. It wins wars, it keeps religions alive, it supports the mental environment we live in. It combats negative thinking, mob mentality, hyper-blame paranoia of mob –consciousness, the fear of opposites.

Positive thinking for some people is angelic thought. Thought that is not provoked into reaction, but into action. Constructive, knowledgeable action, wise action, after decades of inexperienced karma loaded spur of the moment, passionate reaction to spiritual mental energy.

Living as a single person, tests us all. Spiritualists eventually get the picture and choose to keep the idea of romance going, but only to fill the void of need. Perpetual need is survival, hopes and dreams.

Dreams keep us all alive, and everybody dreams,
good and bad dreams, day-dreams, fantasies
(Djin) and angelic daydreams (Angels)

If I had a penny for every reiki healer who came to me for a love reading, I would be a millionaire by now. I tell them why they have rejected living a nuns life. I explain the politics of spiritual existence. To be the hunter of spirit means living with the problems of their customers, living with the promise of earthly love.

Battling with inner worlds, conversations with spirits of earthly pursuits. Need and greed, want and lust. Love and hate and good old stupidity. Dealing with sex addicts in the neighborhood, over-eaters, possessed by what the Chinese call hungry ghosts.

Suicidal depression affecting the sensitive local healers people who are absorbing sick peoples energies. Hyper sensitivity causes over absorbsion of other peoples illnesses.

Denial of lessons learned in the past, release other peoples energies or the beast (i.e. the chemicals produced by our glands) the endorphins we sometimes crave when alternating spirits affect our blood stream will take over as minute disaster cures.

I hear the same argument all the time, " We can have love if we choose to" I always say "Go ahead then, keep the dream alive, go forwards with love."

Ignoring the spiritual realities of this millennium and longer comes with the profession. Becoming a healer means becoming a victim of all that ails your clients. Cheeky self serving self absorbed immature beings with minds open only to dysfunctional spirits and negative controlling forces.

Before you become a healer, you must first become pure and focused on your initial reasons for healing in the first place. Everything that tests you is a spirit of some sort, seeking to infect you as only a virus would. Usually up through your left foot, or the sole of the left foot where as I have observed, energy enters the body. Observations I have made over the decades of spiritual development I have experienced that led me to the last few years of starting to listen to reason.

Trying to get yourself to see things as they really are in a world gone mad willing its own version of reason, the reason of idiots. Eventually you realize that you are meant to be celibate if you're going to be a true, Holy Spirit healer.

The study of Anglican Priests gave me a taste of what sex meant for them. Its was a way to connect with their congregation (No pun intended) making love, or de-stressing from the constant pressure of collective sexual tension. The release from spirits bent on pushing sexual pressure and stress. Also the three day cycle it takes for spiritual people to return to a state of reasonable purity, enough so the energies invoked are not unlike a oriental couple who practice Tantric love-making.

I could feel it from my Anglican neighbors, that once a week they would get it on and in so doing connect with the marriage angels of others on their same wavelength. The wavelength of good karma, people who worship God and temperance. They enjoy an evening of romantic bliss, a state alien to many of my clients, callers and friends. I began to see that some people had good marriages and well balanced non-party mad adolescents. People living in the light of Christ, privileged through good karma. Buddhist-like energies I would love to have achieved in this lifetime, but have myself failed to do so. I'm a single spiritualist, invited to give lectures for the S.N.U.I Spiritualist Union, yet still am surrounded by unhappy lonely psychic mediums and reiki healers stuck in a rut they cannot get out of.

Of course most of us did party hearty in our late teens, or had failed marriages or became addicted to whatever was available. Being an Anglican Priest and being a hermetic healer are obviously two very, very different things. Of course we never see how powerful the art of healing is at first, for the first fifteen years maybe, until we realize, as we rise up the spiritual health ladder, so too do our clients. We are rising up the plains and don't even know it. If it wasn't such hard work, it would be attainable by anyone. Thank God its not.

I mean, otherwise, the village idiot would be charging for his time, maybe he would have his own small business charging us a fool tax and told us "Bum" tax was now mandatory. Life is mandatory and all the fools and jokers that are sent our way because we attract them, are too. Like attracts like, what!

Does that mean we are alikened to useless losers? Yes, yes we are, to a degree, we are human, we are flawed, imperfect, broken, battered and bruised. But we, the good people who do not suffer in silence, learn compassion along the way. Even ex-addicts do, ex-abusive psychotic lunatics become clean, square compassionate and wise if not by learning as to the reasons or the whys of their afflictions, then by therapy.

Anyone can start up a healing business in this world just by being nice. You don't need any certificates like you'll find in the modern world of healers. Just start advertising that you are healing people, sit them down and send them positive energy, love and light. I know of some very successful healers who started this way and have many happy clients.

Of course most of them are married with kids or completely celibate. You can argue with yourself about complications you have experienced after any physical experience in our modern millennium e.t.c. Its obvious to me, something is very, very different and obvious to us all, good and sick/lost/destructive.

The grey area is veering on psychotic, when the madness arrives on your metaphysical door, and the whirling of spiraling karma attacks your mental health.

Boom! Its all on again, Monday to Monday again and again, and the beat goes on. A little older, balder, weaker in the knees after a night of "De-Stressing" Don't worry, you'll recover physically, mentally and spiritually after a couple of days, if its good enough for Anglican bishops, its good enough for you!

The wind is up today. People are moving with it, like cats, we all love cats. The dog people are about too, watery dogs, earthy dogs, Fiery dogs, airy dogs, both men and women. Dog like people are indeed, just that, dog Like. Some say Venusians (People that come from Venus) look like dogs, if you're watching a movie tonight, you may start to see these features in actors faces when the lights are low. Elements have to find their way to our bodies somehow, therefore its inevitable they choose the osmosis of transformation as a platform by which to inhabit humans. Humans under the effects of moral and spiritual states throughout the day, or week e.t.c. Not getting through to you? Woof! Raff! Woof! Woof! Is that better? I thought so.

Gods Dogs, worrying, sniffing, searching, looking for scent, its been around many the year, euphemisms, metaphors. Angels, butterflies, gods, saints, these are metaphors too, we use them daily. No need for repetition when using non-complimentary ones on characters we may name-call once and a while to instigate a reward from our peers, its natural. That's one similarity between animals and humans, peer placement.

In this astral transitional period I have noticed I can no longer pigeonhole my local fools as anything more than numbskull or idiot. If I do, I am attacked rapidly by reprimanding spirits, for using foul language. Every single time I do, I have to hold my astral arms up the Christ and say "please forgive my foul language" and really mean it. That's up to 30 times a day!

You wont have time to argue if you understand me, you will be suffering from the same situation. As a "Seer" which is what we remoter viewers are, we see the disastrous effects of failure, to learn about instant karma. This time period is full of astral spirits, it's the "Jacobs Ladder" of the Millennium. People we have ostracized have become the one thing they tried to recruit others to become, victims of pressured choices, wrong choices. Many of you reading this will have made the same choices I have made, to burn your bridges totally and completely from "Frenemies" Also you're minds are desperately trying to clear away their residual energy.

Disaster number One-One night stands. This is a recent phenomenon, building up force since 2000 (Decades ago). Now if you sleep with someone, your stuck with their astral body or spirit connection for the rest of this lifetime. Your feeling the presence of your divorced husband or wife, you cant get your latest fling out of your head. They seem to be on your mind, a lot. Why? Consequence.

Serious consequence, like using the "N" word at an anti racist demonstration. Or calling The Irish President "Paddy" on the 6 o'clock news. But seriously some people are color blind, deaf and dumb as they come, so not only can you not help them, but your in serious doubt yourself when it comes to the mark. If reiki "Masters" are finding it impossible to become celibate spiritualists its because they have no support network at hand. This book is directed at spiritualists as entertainment and education. For those of you with no attention span that last word I wrote is the only thing on your brain, a brain that is inhabited by ghosts, cobwebs and Black-Hole entities bent on destruction of privacy, sanity and financial security. That's what happens when you forget to test people for light. They are in your aura forever if you never have them cleared. Sleeping with the enemy is no longer an option, but if your meditation is working properly, you'll find your sphincter probably isn't also.

Oxymoron, humans love them, it's the meaning of life! Eventually, you will have enough of suffering, like a lonely soul bending down for the very last time. You will stand up and say "Enough"! I cannot live this way anymore, goodbye old friends, old drinking buddies, old enemies, hello clients, hello your own private office with a waiting-room and a secretary, a solicitor and a life. Or end up in the gutter where your doppelganger doesn't know about consequence, and still yearns for more of the same. Its only a metaphor, is life. Were all endorphin addicts.

Wabam! I make 600 euro's for the first time in the Winter season by getting up at 2.30 am for some reason. Then after 3 complaints by neurotic customers they force me to log in only for 40 hours a week irreguardless to earnings. Story of my life. I felt the devils tingling hands upon my belt. Anyway, after venting my frustration and contemplating mass murder via machete and shotgun, I cooled down, took a xanax and some rhodiola and found my old job with a UK. company for the early hours. Cest la vie!

On and on till the break of dawn. Fighting djin just to stay alive! Djin, a Spirit or Human-like spiritual possession that controls the doppelganger of all humanoids. Its strongest on the weekend especially when its raining. Now I don't usually ditch The Church but the millennium is the return of the unfairly persecuted ones, the old wise women and men of our past.

Many Protestants and Catholics were burned for one reason or another. Its still going on today metaphorically. Unless you're a Tibetan monk or nun , you don't drink, don't smoke and don't have love making sessions at any time of the year especially around the Chinese new year. Unless you join the Hari –Krishna's, actually they do have love making sessions, even though they're married, so they're not really classed as celibate, but they are spiritual beings (Kinda). Its all that food they eat, makes them lively.

You see, if you're stuck at home, working as a tarot reader, or healer, your clients, or patient, in their homes, generally will be in need of help, support and guidance in real time.

Many of them will be all be looking for love or Sex or Sex n Love together. That's the good, normal ones. You on the other hand, may be on a slightly higher Spiritual Path than say, Junkies, Murderers, Rapists, Priests (Joking) Old Ladies with Evil sinners on their minds, losers, weirdo's, perverts and sexual deviants. Impotent middle aged men bent on retarding the minds and confidence of younger men, yes there are men out there that are like this, believe it or not, were not living in a fair society with well balanced educated Middle Class people, contrary to their own b beliefs. Unless you live in Switzerland or Austria.

Your clients are usually in a bit of trouble to say it lightly, even though very hard lessons have been learned, they seem to be blind to education via suffering and are willing to keep going as is.

Well we've come to the end of another book! Wow! How time passes, tonight I am in serene peace, the perfect moment of a perfect day. 1st of October, my favorite month, now I know why the Divil and co. were so active recently, tried to mow me down on the way home (reality)

The year is winding down, the trees are shedding their golden browns and seeds, everybody loves an Indian Summer, momma I'm feeling like I want to follow Autumn around forever. It would be nice to have the opportunity to do so, I suppose I do now that I'm a gypsy tarot reader extraordinaire. Poet philosopher, child of nature, worshipper of the stars and all that appeases the divine. Oh what a gift is discipline, what a wonder is work, work that doesn't feel like work, crystal ball gazing, remote viewing, psychic detective, psychic medium. If I was famous, would it be the destruction of peace and joy? Absolutely.

I suppose some of my customers think I'm sort of famous, but I don't. I'm just a psychic medium making ends meet whilst I spend 183 days a year in one country then another to allude gathering moss!

Paws for thought said the dog to its master, you've been good, that's all that matters, you've avoided temptation during the tempest that is the millennium. You have seen the world, ridden the backs of tsunamis real and imaginary, saved lives and had your own life saved, sometimes by strangers sometimes by your own sweet self. What's the best of the best? Tomorrow is another day! No more Gitanes though!

THE END

9

Printed in Great Britain
by Amazon